# Flask made simple: A Beginner's Guide to Python Web Development

A Beginner-Friendly Guide to Python Web Development

SOMNATH MUKHERJEE

*To the ever-curious minds who seek to create and innovate,*

*To the developers who believe in the beauty of simplicity and elegance in code,*

*And to the open-source community, whose contributions inspire and empower us all.*


*This book is dedicated to you.*


*May your journey with Flask lead to robust applications, impactful projects,*

*and the joy of mastering the art of web development.*

# Contents

# Foreword

In a world where the internet connects everything and everyone, the ability to create web applications has become an essential skill. Python, a language renowned for its simplicity and versatility, has emerged as a favorite among developers. At the heart of Python's web development ecosystem lies Flask—a micro-framework that embodies Python's elegance while empowering developers to build robust, scalable web applications.

Flask Made Simple: Building Your First Python Web App with Flask is more than just a guide; it is a journey. This book has been crafted to simplify the process of learning Flask, even for those new to web development. By focusing on practical examples and clear explanations, it bridges the gap between theory and application, enabling readers to confidently build their first web app by the time they turn the last page.

Whether you are a student exploring web development for the first time, a professional branching into Python, or a hobbyist looking to turn your ideas into reality, this book is your gateway to understanding and mastering Flask. It celebrates the philosophy that learning should be accessible, enjoyable, and empowering.

As you embark on this journey, I encourage you to code along, experiment, and make mistakes—because that is how we grow as developers. With Flask as your tool and this book as your guide, the possibilities are limitless.

Happy coding, and welcome to the world of Flask!

Author

Somnath Mukherjee

Date: 01-01-2025

# Preface

Welcome to "Flask: A Beginner's Guide to Web Development." This book is designed to be your entry point into the world of web application development using Flask, one of Python's most popular and accessible web frameworks. Whether you are a complete beginner to programming or someone with experience in other fields looking to expand your skills into web development, this book has been crafted with you in mind.

Flask stands out among web frameworks for its simplicity and flexibility. It empowers developers to build robust web applications with minimal setup, making it an excellent choice for beginners. By learning Flask, you will not only gain an understanding of the framework itself but also develop essential skills in web development, including routing, templates, databases, and APIs.

The journey through this book is structured to provide a hands-on learning experience. Each chapter introduces core concepts with clear explanations, followed by practical examples and projects that you can build and expand upon. By the end of the book, you will have a solid foundation in Flask and the confidence to create your own web applications.

I believe that learning is most effective when it is both engaging and purposeful. That is why this book emphasizes building real-world applications that solve actual problems. You will create everything from simple "Hello, World!" applications to more complex projects like a blog or a task management tool. Along the way, you will also learn the best practices and tips to help you write clean, maintainable code.

Whether you are learning Flask as a hobby, for a school project, or to enhance your career, this book aims to provide the knowledge and tools you need to succeed. I encourage you to approach each chapter with curiosity and determination. Experiment with the examples, break things, fix them, and, most importantly, have fun while learning.

Thank you for choosing this book as your guide to Flask. Let us embark on this exciting journey together and unlock the power of web development with Python.

The cover of the book is designed by Sumona Mukherjee. Sumona Mukherjee is currently pursuing a Bachelor's degree in Animation and Game Design. She has a strong foundation in graphic design, which enhances her creative and technical skills in her field of study. In addition to her academic pursuits, Sumona works on Fiverr, where she is known for providing reliable and high-quality services. With her dedication, talent, and professionalism, Sumona is steadily building a reputation as a dependable and skilled designer in the creative industry. Her Fiverr link is https://www.fiverr.com/sumonation22/design-custom-icon-set

Somnath Mukherjee

Date: 01-01-2025

# Acknowledgments

This book would not have been possible without the support, inspiration, and contributions of many incredible individuals and communities.

First and foremost, I would like to thank the open-source community, whose tireless dedication to sharing knowledge and building tools has made frameworks like Flask accessible to all. Your contributions remind us of the power of collaboration and the impact of collective innovation.

To my family and friends, thank you for your encouragement, patience, and unwavering belief in my vision. Your support has been my anchor throughout this journey.

A heartfelt thanks to my mentors and colleagues, who have shared their wisdom and helped shape my understanding of Python, Flask, and the art of teaching through writing. Your guidance has been invaluable.

To my readers and learners, you are the reason this book exists. Your curiosity, determination, and enthusiasm for learning inspire me to create content that empowers and educates me.

Finally, to the Flask development team and the Python community, thank you for creating a framework and language that prioritize simplicity, elegance, and developer experience. You have made the journey into web development both enjoyable and rewarding.

This book reflects the collective effort of all these individuals and communities. For that, I am deeply grateful.

With appreciation,

Somnath Mukherjee

# Introduction

The internet is everywhere—on our desktops, in our pockets, and even in our homes. Behind every website, application, and online service lies a web developer who turned an idea into reality. If you have ever wondered how it is done, you are in the right place.

*Flask Made Simple: Building Your First Python Web App with Flask* is your guide to entering the exciting world of web development. This book focuses on Flask, a lightweight and intuitive Python framework that makes building web applications straightforward and enjoyable.

Why Flask? Unlike more complex frameworks, Flask gives you the freedom to build your application your way. It provides the tools you need without dictating how to use them, making it perfect for beginners and flexible enough for advanced projects.

This book is structured to take you from zero to your first fully functional web application. Along the way, you will:

- Learn the basics of Flask and web development.

- Understand how to structure your application for growth and maintainability.

- Dive into key concepts like routing, templates, forms, and databases.

- Gain hands-on experience by building a project step by step.

I have designed this book with simplicity in mind, breaking down each concept into digestible chunks and accompanying them with practical examples. You do not need to be a seasoned programmer to follow along—if you know a little Python and have the desire to learn, you will do great!

By the end of this book, you will have built more than just your first web app. You will have a foundational understanding of Flask and the confidence to take on more ambitious projects.

So, whether you are a student, a hobbyist, or someone transitioning into web development, let us roll up our sleeves and start building. The world of Flask awaits you!

Somnath Mukherjee

# 1. Web Framework

## WF or WAF

A web framework (WF), or web application framework (WAF), is an organized set of tools and code libraries that facilitate the development, deployment, and management of web applications. It provides a unified structure and set of practices for creating robust, scalable, and maintainable applications, helping developers focus on the unique functionality of their projects rather than reinventing foundational elements.

Purpose of Web Frameworks

Web frameworks simplify the process of building web applications by handling common development tasks, such as routing, authentication, and data handling. They provide developers with a streamlined approach to develop applications that meet industry standards, reduce repetitive coding, and address security concerns. The framework essentially provides a skeleton or a backbone on which developers build specific features for their applications.

Core Components and Features

- **Routing and URL Mapping:** Routing is a fundamental feature that allows the application to handle various user requests based on specific URL patterns. In web frameworks, routing helps map URLs to specific actions or controllers. For example, in a blog application, a URL like, "/posts/1" could be mapped to an action that displays a particular blog post. This route allows developers to create friendly, predictable URLs and simplifies the user's experience.

- **Template Engine and Templating Language:** Web frameworks often include a template engine that separates the application's logic from its presentation layer. Template engines use placeholder syntax (for example, Jinja in Flask, EJS in Express.js) to insert dynamic data into HTML pages. This allows for the creation of dynamic web pages that display changing data, such as user profiles, content feeds, or product details, without requiring the developer to hardcode every page variation.

- **Database Abstraction and ORM (Object-Relational Mapping):** Web applications often need to interact with databases, and frameworks typically offer tools for managing these interactions. ORMs allow developers to interact with the database through programming language constructs, making data manipulation more straightforward. For instance, a developer can work with objects in code to represent tables in the database, avoiding the need to write raw SQL. This abstraction also improves security by reducing the risk of SQL injection attacks and allows developers to use the same syntax regardless of the underlying database type.

- **Authentication and Authorization:** User authentication (for example, login and registration) and authorization (for example, access control based on user roles) are common requirements in web applications. Many frameworks offer built-in systems for managing user sessions, securely storing passwords, and restricting access to specific parts of the application. For example, Django has an extensive user authentication system that allows developers to quickly set up login, logout, and permission systems.

- **Security and Protection Against Vulnerabilities:** Security is crucial for web applications, and web frameworks provide built-in protection against common vulnerabilities. For example:

  - **Cross-Site Scripting (XSS):** Sanitizes user input to prevent injection of malicious scripts.

  - **Cross-Site Request Forgery (CSRF):** Add tokens to forms to ensure that requests are intentional.

  - **SQL Injection Protection:** ORMs help prevent malicious SQL queries by using parameterized queries instead of raw SQL.

  These built-in features help reduce security risks and ensure that applications adhere to industry's best practices.

- **Session Management and State Handling:** Web frameworks help manage user sessions, storing information across multiple requests. This allows users to log in, add items to a shopping cart, or save preferences across browsing sessions. Sessions are managed using cookies or other storage methods, and frameworks provide utilities to handle session data securely.

- **Middleware and Plugins:** Many frameworks allow the use of middleware—pieces of code that process requests between the client and server. Middleware can handle tasks like logging, authentication, and data preprocessing. In addition, most frameworks support plugins and modules, which provide additional functionality such as payment processing, email integration, or analytics, allowing developers to enhance the application's features without custom coding.

- **Scalability and Performance Optimization:** Web frameworks often come with tools to optimize performance, such as caching mechanisms, which store frequently accessed data to reduce database queries, and load balancing, which distributes traffic across multiple servers. These features are essential for applications expecting high traffic.


Types of Web Frameworks:

- **Frontend Frameworks:** These frameworks, such as Blazor, React, Angular, and Vue.js, focus on building dynamic, interactive user interfaces. They allow developers to create complex client-side interactions, like single-page applications (SPAs), which enhance user experience by minimizing page reloads.

- **Backend Frameworks:** These frameworks handle server-side processes, database interactions, and APIs. Examples include Django and Flask (Python), Express (Node.js), and Ruby on Rails (Ruby), Dot Net Core WebAPI. Backend frameworks manage data retrieval, business logic, and server-side scripting.

- **Full-Stack Frameworks:** Full-stack frameworks, like ASP.NET and Laravel, provide both frontend and backend components, offering a cohesive environment to manage the entire application stack. This can be beneficial for teams that prefer unified development experience and need tools that support both client and server-side requirements.

Popular Examples of Web Frameworks:

- **Django (Python):** A high-level backend web framework designed to promote rapid development and a clean, pragmatic design. Known for its "batteries-included" philosophy, Django provides many out-of-the-box features like an admin interface, authentication, and an ORM.

- **Flask (Python):** A micro-framework that is lightweight and highly customizable. Flask is often chosen for its simplicity and flexibility, allowing developers to add only the components they need.

- **Ruby on Rails (Ruby):** Rails is known for its "Convention over Configuration" approach, meaning it makes assumptions about the best way to structure and organize code, reducing developer choices and speeding up development.

- **Express.js (Node.js):** A minimal and flexible framework for building server-side applications in JavaScript. It is commonly used in the MERN (MongoDB, Express, React, Node.js) stack for building modern applications.

- **Laravel (PHP):** A full-stack PHP framework known for its elegance and simplicity. Laravel includes tools for authentication, routing, sessions, and caching, with a strong focus on readability and maintainability.

- **ASP.NET (C#):** A robust, enterprise-grade framework for building web applications with C#. It supports both frontend and backend development, making it a popular choice for large, scalable applications.

Benefits of Using Web Frameworks:

- **Accelerated Development:** Web frameworks reduce the amount of code needed for common functionality, making development faster. Frameworks provide tools that automate routine tasks, allowing developers to focus on the unique aspects of their applications.

- **Enhanced Security:** Security is built into many frameworks, with features that help prevent common vulnerabilities. This means developers can trust that their application has a baseline level of security, freeing them to focus on other security needs.

- **Improved Code Organization and Maintainability:** Frameworks provide structured guidelines on how to organize and structure code. This helps developers maintain the codebase as the application grows, reduces errors, and makes collaboration easier.

- **Community Support and Documentation:** Most popular frameworks have strong communities, active support forums, and extensive documentation, making it easy for developers to find help, learn best practices, and stay updated on improvements.

- **Scalability:** Many frameworks include features that make scaling applications simpler, such as load balancing, caching, and database optimization, allowing applications to grow and handle more users over time.

In essence, web frameworks serve as a comprehensive toolkit that aids in developing modern, reliable, and efficient web applications. By providing an organized approach to development, they enable teams to deliver high-quality products faster, with fewer bugs, and with built-in protections against common security issues.

# 2. Flask

Flask is popular for its lightweight web framework in Python. Flask is designed to be simple yet flexible for building web applications. This framework is created by Armin Ronacher in 2010. Often Flask is often called as a "micro-framework" because it is minimalistic by design. This means that it does not require tools or libraries to make it a web framework.

Let us take a closer look at each component of Flask, exploring its design, usage, and application potential in more detail.

## Overview of Flask's Philosophy and Design:

Flask is built around a simple and modular philosophy. It is often termed as a "micro-framework" because it does not impose a lot of dependencies or make assumptions about your project. It provides just the essentials needed to get a web app running, such as routing and templating, but you can easily extend it with plugins or custom code. Flask depends on the **Werkzeug** WSGI toolkit, the **Jinja** template engine, and the **Click** CLI toolkit.

The design of Flask follows the "Werkzeug" and "Jinja2" philosophies:

- **Werkzeug**: It is a Python library for handling HTTP requests and routing. It enables and allows intuitive URL routing and request handling for Flask.

- **Jinja2:** A templating engine that enables and allows to generate HTML with embedded Python code in a secure and efficient way.

**Click**: A Python package designed for creating elegant and efficient command-line interfaces with minimal code. This is also known as the "Command Line Interface Creation Kit," it offers high configurability while providing sensible defaults right out of the box. Click streamlines the development of command-line tools, making the process both quick and enjoyable, while minimizing frustration by ensuring you can easily implement the desired CLI functionality.

- **Core Components of Flask:** Flask relies on a few core components and patterns to help developers build web applications quickly and efficiently:

  - **The Application Object:** The application object (created with **Flask(__name__) )** is the central object of a Flask app, representing the web application and acting as the glue between different parts.

    - You define routes, manage configurations, and run the app through this object.

    - Flask allows customization through configurations, which you can define within the app object.

- **Routing:** Routes are the pathways that users follow to interact with your app. Flask routes are defined using the @app.route() decorator. You can set up dynamic routes with variables in the URL, making it easy to capture user-specific data. Flask routes also support HTTP methods

(GET, POST, etc.), allowing you to specify which method(s) a route should accept. This is particularly useful for handling form submissions or API requests.

- **Request and Response Handling:**
  - Flask provides a `request` object that contains details about the client's request, such as form data, query parameters, headers, and more.
  - Flask also has a `response` object to manage responses to the client, allowing you to set headers, status codes, and content types.

- **Templates and Jinja2 Templating Engine:**
  - Templating engine of Flask, Jinja2, makes it easy to separate HTML structure from Python logic. You can pass data from your Python code to HTML templates, dynamically generating content based on the data.
  - Templates are stored in a templates folder, and Flask uses `render_template` to load them.

- **Error Handling and Debugging:**
  - Flask has a built-in debugging tool, which provides useful error messages during development. When in debug mode, if an error occurs, Flask shows a detailed traceback, helping developers pinpoint issues quickly.
  - Flask also supports custom error handling with functions you can create to handle specific HTTP errors, like `404` or `500`.

- **Working with Databases in Flask:**
  - Flask does not come with built-in database support, which allows developers to choose a solution as per their need.
  - **Flask-SQLAlchemy:** This is the most popular database extension, allowing easy integration with databases through SQLAlchemy, an ORM (Object-Relational Mapper). SQLAlchemy provides a high-level API to interact with databases in Pythonic code.

- **Flask Extensions and Packages:**
  - Flask has a rich ecosystem of extensions that add functionality for a variety of needs:
    - **Flask-WTF:** Simplifies form handling and validation.
    - **Flask-Login:** Manages user sessions, including login/logout and user authentication.
    - **Flask-Migrate:** Handles database migrations, making it easier to update schemas in production.
    - **Flask-RESTful:** Simplifies creating REST APIs, adding tools to help with request handling, serialization, and authentication.

Each extension is integrated seamlessly and follows Flask's design philosophy of modularity, enabling developers to add only what they need.

- **Deployment and Scaling:**
  - Flask apps can be deployed in various environments, from local servers to cloud platforms like Heroku, AWS, and Azure.
  - For larger applications, Flask can work in conjunction with other tools to enhance scalability:
    - **Gunicorn**: A Python WSGI HTTP server that runs Flask in production.
    - **Nginx:** Often used as a reverse proxy to handle more traffic and improve performance.

Flask applications can be containerized with Docker, allowing them to scale more efficiently in cloud environments.

# Flask vs. Django

Flask is often preferred for projects that need quick prototyping or lightweight applications, particularly APIs and microservices.

Django, a heavier, full-featured framework, includes more built-in functionality and is often chosen for larger projects with extensive requirements.

# Use Cases and Applications:

Flask's simplicity and flexibility make it ideal for:

- **Microservices:** Flask's minimalism allows it to be a component within a larger microservices architecture.
- **REST APIs:** Flask can serve as a backend API provider, managing data and business logic for web/mobile applications.
- **Prototyping:** Flask is perfect for quickly developing prototypes and MVPs (Minimum Viable Products).
- **Single-Page Applications (SPAs):** Paired with frontend frameworks, Flask handles the backend while the SPA manages the UI.

Flask is a robust, adaptable framework that enables developers to build powerful web applications and REST APIs with minimal setup, making it a great choice for Python-based web development.

# 3. The Virtual Environment

## Python Environment Builder: Simplifying Development Setup

When working with Python projects, setting up and managing the development environment can often become a challenging task, especially when dealing with multiple projects with varying dependencies. A Python environment builder simplifies this process, ensuring consistency and eliminating potential conflicts.

What is a Python Environment Builder?

A Python environment builder is a tool or script designed to automate the creation, configuration, and management of Python environments. It typically handles:

1.   Virtual Environment Creation: Setting up isolated environments to avoid conflicts between dependencies of different projects.

2.   Dependency Management: Installing the required libraries and packages.

3.   Configuration Management: Setting environment variables, Python versions, and other project-specific settings.

Why use a Python Environment Builder?

1.   **Dependency Isolation**: When working on multiple projects, each may require different versions of libraries or packages. Without a virtual environment, installing one version of a package could cause conflicts with other projects that depend on another version. A virtual environment isolates each project's dependencies, ensuring no conflicts between them.

2.   **Consistency**: Ensures all team members work in the same environment, reducing the "it works on my machine" syndrome.

3.   **Reproducibility**: Virtual environments allow other developers to replicate the same development environment using. When sharing project, can include a '**requirements.txt**' file that lists all dependencies. This helps to create a virtual environment and use this file to install the same dependencies, ensuring the project works similarly on different machines. This makes it easy to replicate the environment on different machines, including CI/CD pipelines. 'pip freeze > requirements.txt', 'pip install -r requirements.txt'
By using the command pip freeze > requirements.txt, creates a file containing the required library.

4.   **Efficiency**: Saves time by automating repetitive setup tasks.

5.   **Clean Environments**: Virtual environments create a separate directory with its own Python executable and directories where the project's specific packages are installed. This ensures your development environment is clean and not cluttered with unnecessary packages that might be installed globally.

If you are a beginner can jump with following topic. Can revisit the topic after learning further.

# Building a Simple Python Environment Builder

Here is a step-by-step guide to creating a basic Python environment builder:

**Step 1: Choose Your Tools**

- **Virtual Environment Tool**: venv, virtualenv, or conda.

- **Dependency Management Tool**: pip, pip-tools, or poetry.

- **Environment Variables**: .env files managed by python-dotenv.

**Step 2: Write a Configuration File**

Use a configuration file like requirements.txt or pyproject.toml to list your dependencies. For example:

**requirements.txt**:

```
flask==2.3.0
requests==2.31.0
python-dotenv==1.0.0
```

In a project if want to create a **requirement.txt**, then by using the command

pip freeze > requirements.txt, creates a file containing the required library.

**Step 3: Automate with a Script**

Below is an example of a Python script for building the environment:

```
import os

import subprocess

def create_virtualenv(env_name):

    if not os.path.exists(env_name):

        subprocess.run(["python", "-m", "venv", env_name])

        print(f"Virtual environment '{env_name}' created.")

    else:

        print(f"Virtual environment '{env_name}' already exists.")

def install_dependencies(env_name, requirements_file):

    subprocess.run([f"{env_name}/bin/pip", "install", "-r", requirements_file])

    print("Dependencies installed.")
```

```python
def setup_environment():

    env_name = "env"

    requirements_file = "requirements.txt"

    create_virtualenv(env_name)

    install_dependencies(env_name, requirements_file)

    print("Environment setup complete.")



if __name__ == "__main__":

    setup_environment()
```

**Step 4: Enhance the Script**

To make the script more robust:

- Add error handling.

- Support multiple configurations (e.g., development and production).

- Automatically load environment variables from a .env file.

**Using Advanced Tools**

If you prefer not to write your own script, consider using advanced tools like:

- **Poetry**: Manages dependencies, environments, and builds.

- **Pipenv**: Combines pip and virtualenv into a single tool.

- **Conda**: Ideal for data science projects and managing complex dependencies.

**Best Practices for Environment Management**

1. **Use Version Control**: Always commit your requirements.txt or pyproject.toml file.

2. **Isolate Projects**: Create a new virtual environment for every project.

3. **Document the Setup**: Provide clear instructions or scripts for replicating the environment.

# For beginners:

For this book the Visual Studio Code is being used for understanding example codes.

Create a Folder of your own choice, for this book a folder named tutorial is used.

Open the Folder [tutorial] as show in the picture.

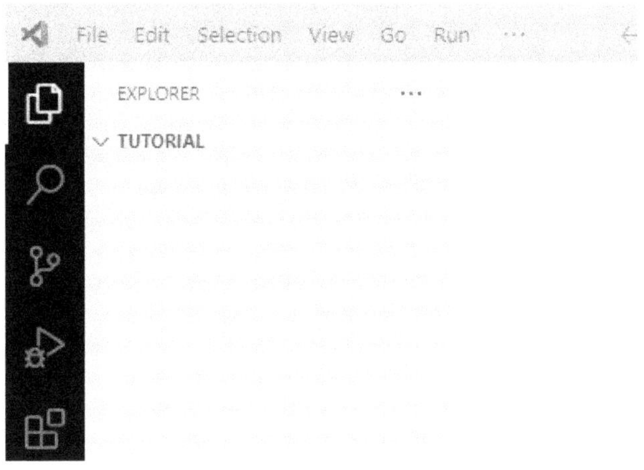

# Install virtualenv for development environment

virtualenv is a virtual Python environment builder. It helps a user to create multiple Python environments side-by-side. Thereby, it can avoid compatibility issues between the different versions of the libraries.

The following command installs virtualenv. This command needs administrator privileges.

pip install virtualenv

Or

py -3 -m venv .venv

Then open a new terminal

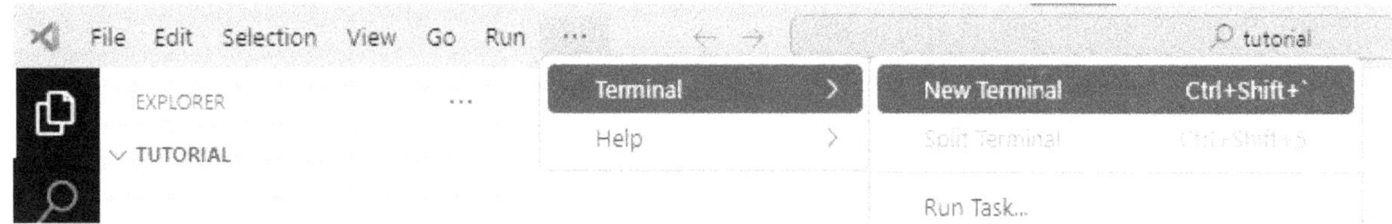

To activate corresponding environment, following can be used

.venv\scripts\activate

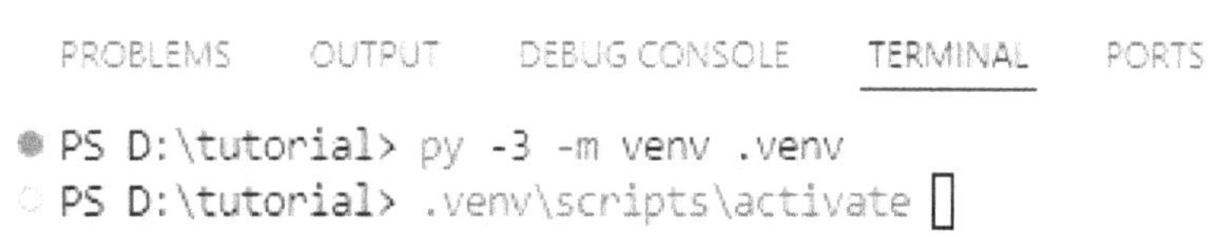

We are now ready to install Flask in this environment.

pip install Flask

The above command can be run directly, without virtual environment for system-wide installation.

```
PROBLEMS    OUTPUT    DEBUG CONSOLE    TERMINAL    PORTS

● PS D:\tutorial> py -3 -m venv .venv
● PS D:\tutorial> .venv\scripts\activate
  (.venv) PS D:\tutorial> pip install Flask []
```

```
PROBLEMS    OUTPUT    DEBUG CONSOLE    TERMINAL    PORTS

Using cached flask-3.1.0-py3-none-any.whl (102 kB)
Using cached blinker-1.9.0-py3-none-any.whl (8.5 kB)
Using cached click-8.1.8-py3-none-any.whl (98 kB)
Using cached itsdangerous-2.2.0-py3-none-any.whl (16 kB)
Using cached jinja2-3.1.5-py3-none-any.whl (134 kB)
Using cached werkzeug-3.1.3-py3-none-any.whl (224 kB)
Using cached MarkupSafe-3.0.2-cp312-cp312-win_amd64.whl (15 kB)
Using cached colorama-0.4.6-py2.py3-none-any.whl (25 kB)
Installing collected packages: MarkupSafe, itsdangerous, colorama, blinker, Werkzeug, Jinja2, click, Flask
Successfully installed Flask-3.1.0 Jinja2-3.1.5 MarkupSafe-3.0.2 Werkzeug-3.1.3 blinker-1.9.0 click-8.1.8 colo

[notice] A new release of pip is available: 23.2.1 -> 24.3.1
[notice] To update, run: python.exe -m pip install --upgrade pip
(.venv) PS D:\tutorial> []
```

# 4. The Application

To test Flask installation, type the following code in the editor as Hello.py

```python
from flask import Flask

app = Flask(__name__)


@app.route('/')

def hello_world():

    return 'Hello World'


if __name__=='__main__':

    app.run()
```

```
Welcome          hello.py    ×
hello.py > ...
3      app =Flask(__name__)
4
5      @app.route('/')
6      def hello_world():
7          return 'Hello World'
8
9      if __name__ == '__main__':
10         app.run()
```

    Importing flask module in the project is mandatory. This enables an object of Flask class is to make a WSGI application. WSGI stands for Web Server Gateway Interface, and it is a standard interface that allows web servers to communicate with Python web applications.

    Flask constructor takes the name of current module (__name__) as argument.

    The route() function of the Flask class is a decorator, which tells the application which URL should call the associated function.  The syntax is:

app.route(rule, options)

    In the above example, '/' URL is bound with hello_world() function. Hence, when the home page of web server is opened in browser, the output of this function will be rendered.

Finally the run() method of Flask class runs the application on the local development server.

```
app.run(host, port, debug, options)
```

A **Flask** application is started by calling the **run()** method.

The rule parameter represents URL binding with the function.

Detailed explanation and example are provided in the next chapter dedicated for Routing.

The above given Python script is executed from Python shell.

Python Hello.py

```
PROBLEMS    OUTPUT    DEBUG CONSOLE    TERMINAL    PORTS

(.venv) PS D:\tutorial> python hello.py
 * Serving Flask app 'hello'
 * Debug mode: off
WARNING: This is a development server. Do not use it in a production deployment. Use a production WSGI server instead.
 * Running on http://127.0.0.1:5000
Press CTRL+C to quit
```

List of parameters and description could be used

| S No. | Parameter | Description |
| --- | --- | --- |
| 1 | host | Hostname to listen on. Defaults to 127.0.0.1 (localhost). Set to '0.0.0.0' to have server available externally |
| 2 | port | Defaults to 5000 |
| 3 | debug | Defaults to false. If set to true, provides a debug information |
| 4 | options | To be forwarded to underlying Werkzeug server. |

A message in Python shell informs that

* Running on http://127.0.0.1:5000/ (Press CTRL+C to quit)

Open the above URL **(localhost:5000)** in the browser. **'Hello World'** message will be displayed on it.

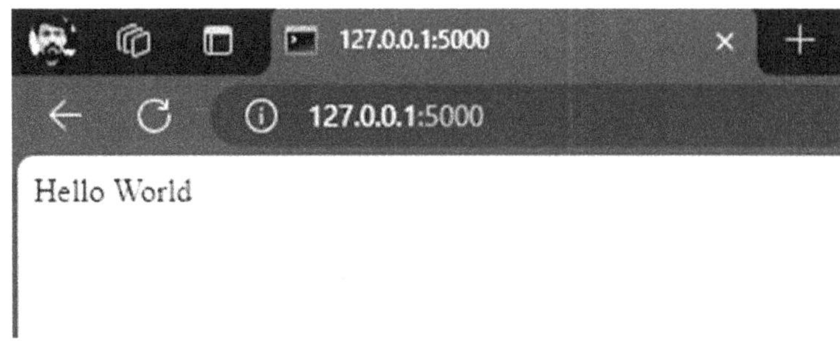

# Debug mode

While the application is under development, it should be restarted manually for each change in the code. To avoid this inconvenience, enable **debug support**. The server will then reload itself if the code changes. It will also provide a useful debugger to track the errors if any, in the application.

The **Debug** mode is enabled by two different ways. One setting the **debug** property of the **application** object to **True** before running. Another by passing the debug parameter to the **run()** method.

One Way:

```
app.debug = True

app.run()
```

Another Way:

```
app.run(debug = True)
```

# 5. The Routing

Routing in Flask is the mechanism that maps URL patterns to specific view functions, enabling a web application to respond to user requests with appropriate data or actions. Flask's routing system is both powerful and easy to use, providing flexibility for defining application behaviour.

The web frameworks use the routing technique to help a user remember application URLs. It is useful to access the desired page directly without having to navigate from the home page.

## Key Concepts

1. **Route Decorator:**

   - Flask uses the @app.route() decorator to bind a URL to a Python function.

```python
1  from flask import Flask
2  app = Flask(__name__)
3
4  @app.route('/')
5  def home():
6      return "Welcome to the homepage!"
7
8  if __name__ == '__main__':
9      app.run(debug=True)
```

2. **Dynamic Routing:**

   - Flask allows you to define dynamic parts in the route using angle brackets < >.

```python
8  @app.route('/user/<username>')
9  def show_user_profile(username):
10     return f"User: {username}"
```

   - You can also specify variable types:

```python
12  @app.route('/post/<int:post_id>')
13  def show_post(post_id):
14      return f"Post ID: {post_id}"
```

   - Supported types:
     - string (default)
     - int
     - float
     - path (like string but allows slashes /)

- uuid

3. HTTP Methods:

- By default, routes only respond to GET requests.

- To allow other methods like POST, PUT, or DELETE, specify the methods parameter in the decorator.

```
16  @app.route('/submit', methods=['GET', 'POST'])
17  def submit():
18      if request.method == 'POST':
19          return "Data submitted!"
20      return "Submit your data."
```

4. URL Building:

- Flask provides url_for() to dynamically build URLs.

```
1   from flask import Flask, url_for
2
3   app = Flask(__name__)
4
5   @app.route('/login')
6   def login():
7       return "Login Page"
8
9   @app.route('/profile')
10  def profile():
11      return url_for('login')  # Returns "/login"
12
13  if __name__ == '__main__':
14      app.run(debug=True)
```

5. Route Customization:

- Routes can have custom behaviours, such as trailing slashes or unique converters.

  - Adding a trailing slash (/route/) makes the route more forgiving.

  - Omitting the slash (/route) enforces strict matching.

```
13  @app.route('/route/')
14  def my_route():
15      return "Route with trailing slash!"
16
```

6. Static Files:

- Flask serves static files (e.g., CSS, JavaScript, images) using the /static route.

- Place static files in a folder named static by default or customize the location.

7. Error Handling:

- Flask allows you to define custom error pages for different HTTP errors using error handlers.

```
16
17  @app.errorhandler(404)
18  def page_not_found(e):
19      return "Page not found!", 404
20
```

# 6. The rules for Variable

When working with Flask, understanding the rules and best practices for defining, managing, and using variables in both your Python code and Flask templates is crucial. Here is a detailed breakdown of variable rules in Flask:

1. Variables in Flask Routes:

    a. Defining Variables in Routes:

        i. Flask allows you to define routes with dynamic variables in the URL. These variables are captured and passed as arguments to the associated view function.

```
4  @app.route('/user/<username>')
5  def show_user(username):
6      return f'User: {username}'
7
```

    b. Supported Variable Types:

        i. Flask supports type conversion for route variables by using the <type:variable> syntax.

        ii. Types:

            1. string (default): Accepts any string without a /.

            2. int: Accepts integers.

            3. float: Accepts floating-point numbers.

            4. path: Like string but accepts /.

            5. uuid: Accepts UUID strings.

```
8   @app.route('/post/<int:post_id>')
9   def show_post(post_id):
10      return f'Post ID: {post_id}'
11
```

    c. URL Building with Variables:

        i. Use url_for() to dynamically build URLs with variables:

```
  variable002.py  ×
  variable002.py > ...
   1   from flask import Flask, url_for
   2
   3   app = Flask(__name__)
   4
   5   @app.route('/user/<username>')
   6   def show_user(username):
   7       return f'Hello {username}'
   8
   9   # In another function or template
  10   url_for('show_user', username='Somnath')
  11   # Output: /user/Somnath
  12
  13
  14   if __name__ == '__main__':
  15       app.run(debug=True)
```

2.  Flask Template Variables:

    a.  Passing Variables to Templates:

        i.  Flask uses the **Jinja2** templating engine, where variables passed from the view function are accessible in templates.

```
  variable003.py  ×
  variable003.py > ...
   1   from flask import Flask, render_template
   2
   3   app = Flask(__name__)
   4
   5   @app.route('/greet/<name>')
   6   def greet(name):
   7       return render_template('variable003.html', name=name)
   8
   9   if __name__ == '__main__':
  10       app.run(debug=True)
  11
```

        ii.  Make sure that the template file variable003.html placed in a folder called templates.

```
  variable003.py        <> variable003.html  ×
  templates > <> variable003.html > @ p
   1   <p>Hello, {{ name }}!</p>
```

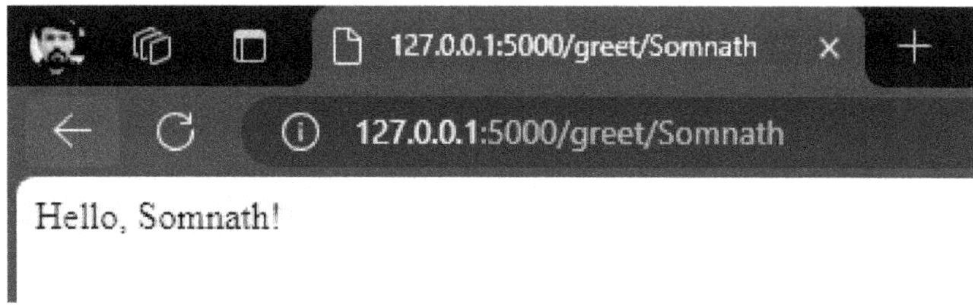


b. Variable Scoping in Templates:

    i. Variables passed to templates are specific to that rendering context.

    ii. Multiple variables can be passed to templates.

```python
from flask import Flask, render_template

app = Flask(__name__)

@app.route('/greet/<name>')
def greet(name):
    id = 10
    return render_template('variable004.html', id=id, name=name)

if __name__ == '__main__':
    app.run(debug=True)
```

```html
<p>User ID: {{ id }}</p>
<p>Upper Name: {{ name.upper() }}</p>
```

c. Accessing Attributes and Methods:

    i. Use dot notation to access object attributes or methods.

```html
<p>User ID: {{ user.id }}</p>
<p>Upper Name: {{ user.name.upper() }}</p>
```

Here **user** is an object created from a model, will discuss later in this book.

d. Default Values for Variables:

    i. Use Jinja2 filters like default to handle undefined variables:

```html
<p>{{ name | default('Guest') }}</p>
```

3. Global Variables:

    a. Using **g** for Application Context Variables:

        i. Flask provides the g object to store data globally for a single request context.

    b. Avoid Overuse.

        i. Use g sparingly to avoid tightly coupling different parts of the app.

4. Environment Variables:

    a. Setting Environment Variables:

        i. Flask uses environment variables for configuration (e.g., FLASK_ENV, FLASK_DEBUG).

        ii. For example bash command: export FLASK_ENV=development

    b. Accessing Environment Variables:

        i. Use the **os** module to access custom environment variables.

```python
from flask import Flask, g
import os

app = Flask(__name__)

SECRET_KEY = os.getenv('SECRET_KEY', 'default_key')
```

**Moreover: Another way.**

```python
def anotherway():
    return 'This is another way to add url'


app.add_url_rule('/anotherway', 'anotherway', anotherway)


@app.route('/user/<name>')
def user(name):
    # return 'Welcome '+ name +' to our website.'
    return 'Welcome %s to our website.' % name


if __name__ == '__main__':
    app.run(debug = True)
```

In addition to the default string variable part, rules can be constructed using the following converters:

| S No | Converters | Description |
| --- | --- | --- |
| 1 | **int** | Accepts integer |
| 2 | **float** | For floating point value |
| 3 | **path** | Accepts slashes used as directory separator character |

In the following code, all these constructors are used.

**exampleurl.py**

```python
from flask import Flask

app = Flask(__name__)

@app.route('/eggs/<int:dozen>')

def show_blog(dozen):

    return 'Wanted to purchase %d of eggs.' % dozen

@app.route('/price/<float:amount>')

def revision(amount):

    return 'Purchase price is %f' % amount

if __name__ == '__main__':

  app.run()
```

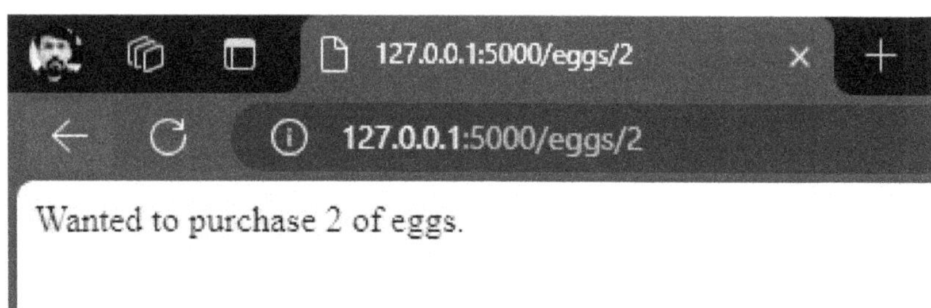

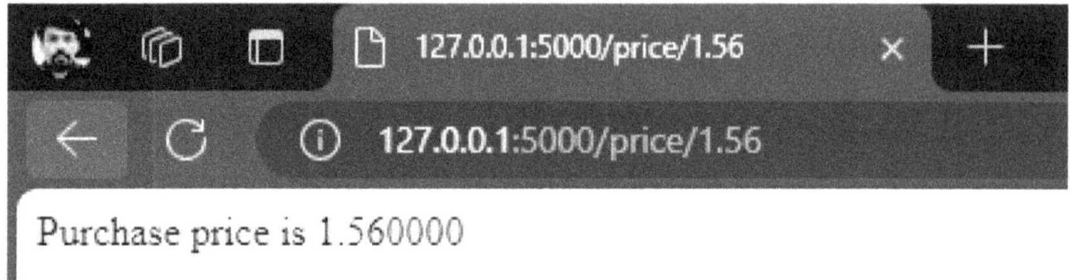


Purchase price is 1.560000

# 7. The URL Building

The **url_for()** function in Flask is a key feature that allows developers to generate URLs dynamically in their application. Rather than hardcoding URLs, url_for() uses the names of view functions to build URLs, ensuring that changes to route definitions automatically propagate throughout the application. This approach enhances maintainability, consistency, and flexibility. The function accepts the name of a function as first argument, and one or more keyword arguments, each corresponding to the variable part of URL.

## How url_for() Works

The url_for() function looks up the URL rule associated with a given endpoint (the name of the view function) and returns the corresponding URL. It also accepts arguments to populate dynamic URL parts or add query parameters.

## Anatomy of url_for()

url_for(endpoint, **values)

- Parameters:
    - endpoint:
        - A string representing the name of the view function tied to the route.
        - This is the primary identifier for the route in the Flask application.
    - **values:
        - Key-value pairs used to fill placeholders in the URL or add query parameters.
        - Dynamic arguments in routes are specified as keyword arguments.
        - Special arguments like _external and _scheme modify URL generation.

Why Use url_for()?

- **Dynamic URL Generation**: Automatically updates URLs when routes change.

- **Reverse URL Lookup**: Generates URLs based on the function names of the routes.

- **Maintainability**: Avoids hardcoding URLs, reducing errors when paths change.

- **Flexibility**: Adds query parameters and handles arguments seamlessly.

Features and Use Cases:

1. Static URLs:

   a. Generates a URL for a static route.

```python
from flask import Flask, url_for

app = Flask(__name__)

@app.route('/')
def index():
    url_for('home')  # Output: '/home'

@app.route('/home')
def home():
    return 'Welcome to Home'

if __name__ == '__main__':
    app.run(debug=True)
```

In the above example on visiting the index url, it will automatically transfer to the home page as instructed in the code of 7th line.

2. Dynamic URLs:

   a. Handles routes with placeholders.

```python
from flask import Flask, url_for, redirect
app = Flask(__name__)

@app.route('/user/<username>')
def profile(username):
    if username =='admin':
        return redirect(url_for('hello_admin'))
    else:
        return redirect(url_for('hello_guest', guest = username))

@app.route('/admin')
def hello_admin():
    return 'Hello Admin'

@app.route('/guest/<guest>')
def hello_guest(guest):
    return 'Hello %s' % guest

if __name__ == '__main__':
    app.run(debug=True)
```

On entering url http://127.0.0.1:5000/user/admin

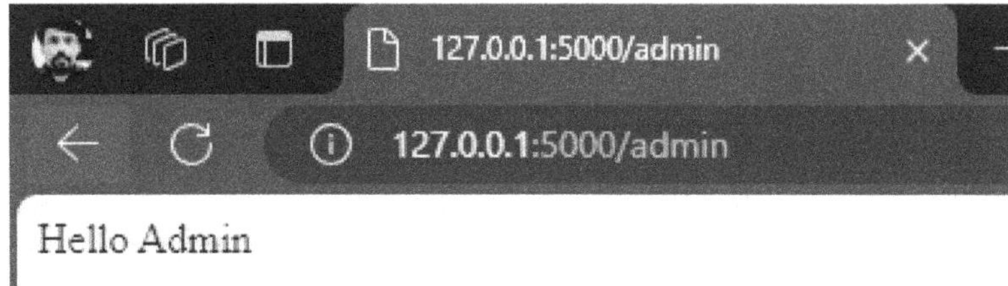

On entering url http://127.0.0.1:5000/user/somnath

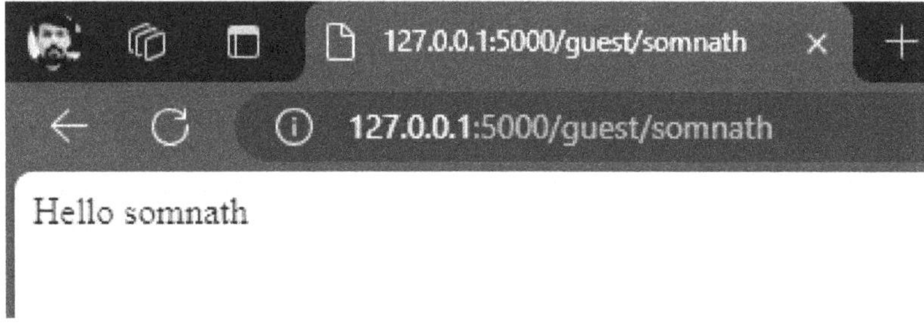

3. Query Parameters:

   a. Appends GET query strings by passing additional keyword arguments.

```python
from flask import Flask, url_for, redirect
app = Flask(__name__)


@app.route('/test')
def test():
    return redirect(url_for('home', page=2, filter='active'))
    # Output: '/home?page=2&filter=active'


@app.route('/home/<page>/<filter>')
def home(page, filter):
    return 'Page No ' +  page + ' filter is '+filter


if __name__ == '__main__':
    app.run(debug=True)
```

On entering the url http://127.0.0.1:5000/test

Page No 2 filter is active

4. Static Files:

   a. Serves static files using the built-in static endpoint.

```
url_for('static', filename='main.js')
# Output: '/static/main.js'
```

    b.  Will be discussed later in this book.

5.  Absolute URLs:

    a.  Generates a full URL with domain and scheme using _external=True.

```
url_for('home', _external=True)
# Output: 'http://localhost:5000/home'
```

    b.  Will be discussed later in this book.

6.  Custom URL Schemes:

    a.  Modifies the scheme for the URL (e.g., switching to HTTPS).

```
url004.py  ×

url004.py > ...
1    from flask import Flask, url_for, redirect
2    app = Flask(__name__)
3
4    @app.route('/test')
5    def test():
6        return redirect(url_for('home', _external=True, _scheme='https'))
7        # Output: 'https://localhost:5000/home'
8
9    @app.route('/home')
10   def home():
11       return 'Home Page.'
12
13   if __name__ == '__main__':
14       app.run(debug=True)
15
```

On entering the url http://127.0.0.1:5000/test

*Using url_for() in Templates*

Flask's url_for() integrates seamlessly with Jinja2 templates, simplifying dynamic URL generation.

Example:

```
url005.py  ✕    <> url005.html

url005.py > index
1    from flask import Flask, render_template
2    app = Flask(__name__)
3
4    @app.route("/")
5    def index():
6        return render_template('url005.html')
7
8    @app.route('/product/<int:product_id>')
9    def product_detail(product_id):
10       return f'Product {product_id}'
11
12   if __name__ == '__main__':
13       app.run(debug=True)
14
```

```
url005.py      <> url005.html  ✕

templates > <> url005.html > ...
1    <a href="{{ url_for('product_detail', product_id=123) }}">View Product</a>
2
```

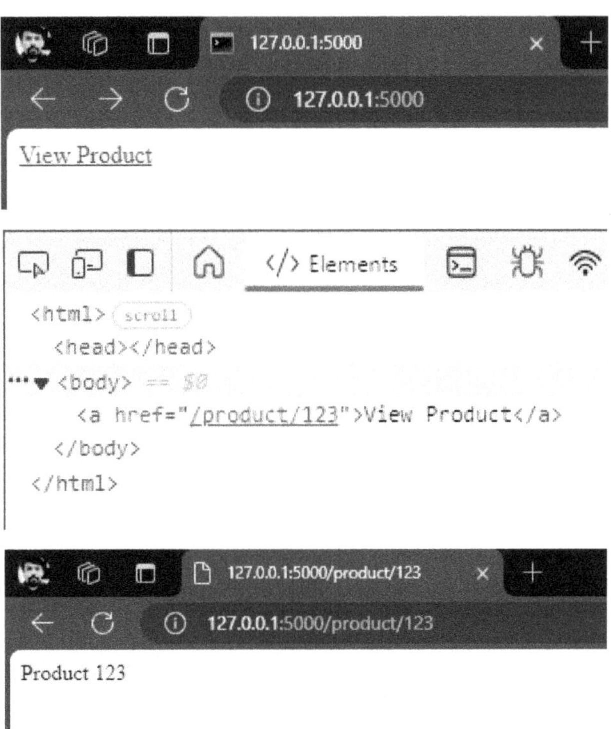



Advanced Features:

1. **Subdomains:**

    a.  Flask supports subdomain routing. Use the subdomain argument in url_for().

```python
from flask import Flask, url_for, redirect
app = Flask(__name__)
app.config['SERVER_NAME'] = 'example.com'


@app.route('/user/<username>', subdomain='<subdomain>')
def subdomain_user(subdomain, username):
    return f'{username} on {subdomain}'


@app.route('/test')
def test():
    url_for('subdomain_user', subdomain='blog', username='Alice', _external=True)
    # Output: 'http://blog.example.com/user/Alice'



if __name__ == '__main__':
    app.run(debug=True)
```

2. **Testing URLs Without Running the Server**:

   a. Use app.test_request_context() to test URL generation during development.

   ```python
   with app.test_request_context():
       print(url_for('home'))   # Output: '/home'
   ```

3. **Support for Blueprint Routes**:

   a. In applications with Blueprints, use the blueprint-qualified function name.

   ```python
   url_for('blueprint_name.function_name')
   ```

Will discuss later in this book.

Error Handling:

1. Missing Endpoint:

   a. If the endpoint doesn't exist, Flask raises a BuildError.

   ```python
   url_for('nonexistent')
   # werkzeug.routing.BuildError: Could not build URL for endpoint 'nonexistent'.
   ```

Will discuss later in this book.

2. Missing Required Parameters:

   a. Routes with placeholders require corresponding arguments in url_for().

```python
@app.route('/user/<username>')
def profile(username):
    return f'User {username}'

url_for('profile')
# werkzeug.routing.BuildError: Could not build URL for endpoint 'profile' with values ['username'].
```

Best Practices

1. Avoid Hardcoding URLs

    a. Always use url_for() to ensure that URLs remain consistent and updates to route paths are automatically reflected.

2. Meaningful View Function Names

    a. Use descriptive names for your view functions to make url_for() calls intuitive.

3. Test Thoroughly:

    a. Use app.test_request_context() during development to verify URL generation logic.

4. Handle Static Files:

    a. Serve static resources using url_for('static') to avoid hardcoding paths.

5. Combine with Template Logic:

    a. Use url_for() in Jinja2 templates for cleaner and more dynamic link generation.


Example:

```
url007.py  ×

url007.py > ...
  1    from flask import Flask, url_for
  2
  3    app = Flask(__name__)
  4
  5    @app.route('/')
  6    def index():
  7        return 'Home Page'
  8
  9    @app.route('/profile/<username>')
 10    def profile(username):
 11        return f'Welcome, {username}!'
 12
 13    @app.route('/search')
 14    def search():
 15        return 'Search Page'
 16
 17    if __name__ == '__main__':
 18        app.run(debug=True)
```

```
with app.test_request_context():
    print(url_for('index'))  # Output: '/'
    print(url_for('profile', username='Alice'))  # Output: '/profile/Alice'
    print(url_for('search', q='flask'))  # Output: '/search?q=flask'
```

Output:

```
/
/profile/Alice
/search?q=flask
/
/profile/Alice
/search?q=flask
```

# 8. The HTTP methods

## Understanding HTTP Methods in Flask:

Flask provides an intuitive and flexible way to handle HTTP methods. These methods dictate the type of action a server should perform, making them essential for building web applications and APIs. Let us explore the various HTTP methods and how they are implemented in Flask.

What Are HTTP Methods?

HTTP methods define the operations allowed on a resource. They are part of the HTTP protocol used for communication between clients and servers. The commonly used methods include:

- **GET**: Retrieve data from the server.

- **POST**: Send data to the server to create or update a resource.

- **PUT**: Update an entire resource.

- **DELETE**: Remove a resource from the server.

- **PATCH**: Partially update a resource.

Using HTTP Methods in Flask

Flask makes it easy to handle these methods by specifying them in route decorators. Let us break down each method with examples.

1. **Handling GET Requests:**

   - GET requests are used to fetch data or render pages. These requests are stateless and should not modify any data on the server.

```python
from flask import Flask, request
app = Flask(__name__)


# Example usage: /greet?name=Somnath
@app.route('/greet', methods=['GET'])
def greet():
    name = request.args.get('name', 'Guest')
    return f"Hello, {name}!"

if __name__ == '__main__':
    app.run(debug=True)
```

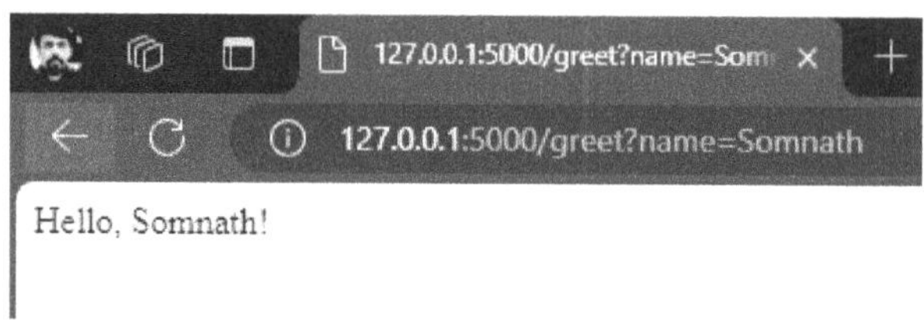


## 2. Handling POST Requests:

- POST requests are used to send data to the server, typically to create or update resources. Form data and JSON payloads are common in POST requests.

```python
from flask import Flask, request
app = Flask(__name__)

@app.route('/submit', methods=['POST'])
def submit():
    name = request.form.get('name')
    return f"Name submitted: {name}"

@app.route('/api/data', methods=['POST'])
def api_data():
    data = request.json
    return f"Received JSON: {data}"


if __name__ == '__main__':
    app.run(debug=True)
```

## 3. Handling PUT Requests:

- PUT requests are used to update an entire resource. This is often used in REST APIs for modifying existing data.

```python
from flask import Flask, request
app = Flask(__name__)

@app.route('/update/<int:id>', methods=['PUT'])
def update_resource(id):
    data = request.json
    return f"Resource {id} updated with data: {data}"

if __name__ == '__main__':
    app.run(debug=True)
```

4. **Handling DELETE Requests:**

   - DELETE requests remove resources from the server. Ensure proper authentication and validation when implementing this method to prevent accidental deletions.

```python
@app.route('/delete/<int:id>', methods=['DELETE'])
def delete_resource(id):
    return f"Resource {id} deleted"
```

5. **Handling PATCH Requests:**

   - PATCH requests are used to partially update a resource. This method is efficient when only specific fields need to be modified.

```python
@app.route('/patch/<int:id>', methods=['PATCH'])
def patch_resource(id):
    data = request.json
    return f"Resource {id} partially updated with: {data}"
```

# Combining Methods in a Single Route

Flask allows you to handle multiple methods for a single route by specifying them in the methods parameter.

```python
# http004.py > ...
1   from flask import Flask, request
2   app = Flask(__name__)
3
4   @app.route('/multi', methods=['GET', 'POST'])
5   def multi():
6       if request.method == 'GET':
7           return "This is a GET request."
8       elif request.method == 'POST':
9           return "This is a POST request."
10
11  if __name__ == '__main__':
12      app.run(debug=True)
13
14
```

Best Practices for Using HTTP Methods in Flask

1. **Explicit Method Declaration:** Always specify the methods explicitly in the route decorators to avoid ambiguity.

2. **Input Validation:** Validate and sanitize user inputs to prevent security vulnerabilities like SQL injection or XSS.

3. **Error Handling**: Implement proper error handling using Flask's abort function for invalid inputs or unauthorized access.

4. **RESTful Design**: Follow RESTful principles to create intuitive and predictable APIs.

5. **Flask Extensions**: Use Flask extensions like **Flask-RESTful** or **Flask-SQLAlchemy** for better structure and scalability.

Example:

```python
from flask import Flask, redirect, url_for, request
app = Flask(__name__)
@app.route('/')
def index():
 return '''<html>
 <body>
 <form action = "http://localhost:5000/login" method = "post">
 <p>Enter Name:</p>
 <p><input type = "text" name = "nm" /></p>
 <p><input type = "submit" value = "submit" /></p>
 </form>
 </body>
 </html>'''


@app.route('/success/<name>')
def success(name):
    return 'Welcome %s' % name


@app.route('/login', methods = ['POST', 'GET'])
def login():
    if request.method == 'POST':
        user = request.form['nm'] + " POST"
        return redirect(url_for('success', name = user))
    else:
        user = request.args.get('nm') + " Get"
        return redirect(url_for('success', name = user))


if __name__ == '__main__':
    app.run(debug = True)
```

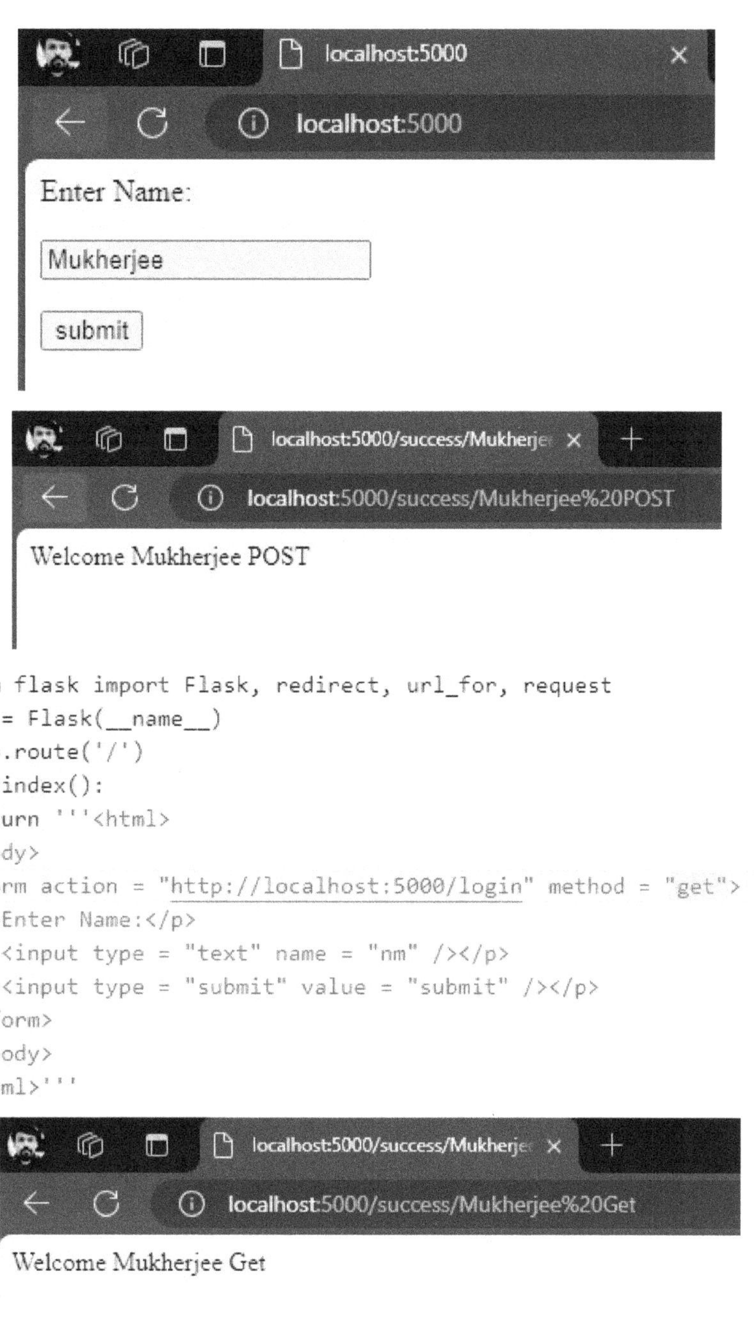

```python
from flask import Flask, redirect, url_for, request
app = Flask(__name__)
@app.route('/')
def index():
 return '''<html>
 <body>
 <form action = "http://localhost:5000/login" method = "get">
 <p>Enter Name:</p>
 <p><input type = "text" name = "nm" /></p>
 <p><input type = "submit" value = "submit" /></p>
 </form>
 </body>
</html>'''
```

# 9. The Templates

Flask provides a powerful templating engine called **Jinja2**. Templates in Flask are used to dynamically generate HTML, making it easy to separate application logic from presentation. It is possible to return the output of a function bound to a certain URL in the form of HTML.

For instance, in the following script, **index()** function will render 'Hello World' with **<h1>** tag attached to it.

```
template001.py  ×

template001.py > ...
  1   from flask import Flask
  2   app = Flask(__name__)
  3
  4   @app.route('/')
  5   def index():
  6       return '<html><body><h1>Hello World</h1></body></html>'
  7
  8   if __name__ == '__main__':
  9       app.run(debug = True)
 10
```

However, generating HTML content from Python code is cumbersome, especially when variable data and Python language elements like conditionals or loops need to be put. This would require frequent escaping from HTML.

## What is a Template in Flask?

A template in Flask is an HTML file with placeholders for dynamic content. These placeholders use the Jinja2 syntax, allowing developers to include logic like loops and conditionals within the HTML.

## Creating a Template

1.  Set Up Your Flask Application:

```
template002.py  ×     <> index.html

template002.py > home
  1   from flask import Flask, render_template
  2
  3   app = Flask(__name__)
  4
  5   @app.route("/")
  6   def home():
  7       return render_template("index.html", title="Welcome", name="Somnath")
  8
  9   if __name__ == "__main__":
 10       app.run(debug=True)
 11
```

2. Create a Templates Folder By default, Flask looks for templates in a directory named templates in the root of your project.

3. Write the Template File Create an index.html file in the templates folder.

```
template002.py          <> index.html  ×

templates > <> index.html > ...
    1    <!DOCTYPE html>
    2    <html lang="en">
    3    <head>
    4        <meta charset="UTF-8">
    5        <meta name="viewport" content="width=device-width, initial-scale=1.0">
    6        <title>{{ title }}</title>
    7    </head>
    8    <body>
    9        <h1>Hello, {{ name }}!</h1>
    10       <p>Welcome to the Flask app.</p>
    11   </body>
    12   </html>
    13
```

# Hello, Somnath!

Welcome to the Flask app.

## Dynamic Content with Placeholders

Placeholders in Jinja2 are wrapped in double curly braces {{ ... }}. They allow you to insert dynamic content into the HTML.

Example: The year.html page may have: <p>The current year is {{ year }}</p>

```
@app.route("/year")
def year():
    current_year = datetime.now().year
    return render_template("year.html", year=current_year)
```

The **jinja2** template engine uses the following delimiters for escaping from HTML.

- {% ... %} for Statements

- {{ ... }} for Expressions to print to the template output

- {# ... #} for Comments not included in the template output

- # ... ## for Line Statements

# Control Structures

Jinja2 supports control structures like loops and conditionals:

**Loops:**

```
template003.py ×    <> items.html
template003.py > items
1    from flask import Flask, render_template
2
3    app = Flask(__name__)
4
5    @app.route("/items")
6    def items():
7        shopping_list = ["Apples", "Bananas", "Cherries"]
8        return render_template("items.html", items=shopping_list)
9
10   if __name__ == "__main__":
11       app.run(debug=True)
12
```

```
template003.py       <> items.html ×
templates > <> items.html > ul
1    <ul>
2        {% for item in items %}
3        <li>{{ item }}</li>
4        {% endfor %}
5    </ul>
```

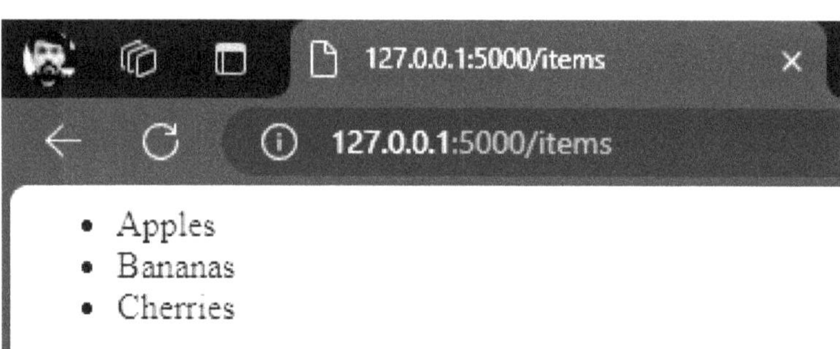



**Conditionals:**

```python
template004.py  ×     <> dashboard.html

template004.py > ...
 1    from flask import Flask, render_template
 2
 3    app = Flask(__name__)
 4
 5    @app.route("/loggedin/<username>")
 6    def items(username):
 7        return render_template("dashboard.html", user_logged_in='1', username="Somnath")
 8
 9    if __name__ == "__main__":
10        app.run(debug=True)
```

```html
template004.py        <> dashboard.html  ×

templates > <> dashboard.html > ...
 1    {% if user_logged_in %}
 2        <p>Welcome back, {{ username }}!</p>
 3    {% else %}
 4        <p>Please log in.</p>
 5    {% endif %}
```



# Template Inheritance

Template inheritance allows you to define a base template with common structures and extend it in other templates. Template inheritance is a feature of Flask's Jinja2 templating engine that allows developers to create a base template with common structures (like headers, footers, and navigation menus) and extend it in child templates. This technique ensures consistent layouts across pages and improves maintainability by reducing redundancy.

**How Template Inheritance Works**

1. **Base Template**
   The base template defines the common layout or structure for the application. It uses **blocks** as placeholders for dynamic content that child templates can override.

```html
<!-- base.html -->
<!DOCTYPE html>
<html lang="en">
<head>
    <meta charset="UTF-8">
    <meta name="viewport" content="width=device-width, initial-scale=1.0">
```

```html
    <title>{% block title %}Default Title{% endblock %}</title>
    <link rel="stylesheet" href="{{ url_for('static', filename='styles.css') }}">
</head>
<body>
    <header>
        <h1>My Application</h1>
        <nav>
            <ul>
                <li><a href="/">Home</a></li>
                <li><a href="/about">About</a></li>
                <li><a href="/contact">Contact</a></li>
            </ul>
        </nav>
    </header>
    <main>
        {% block content %}{% endblock %}
    </main>
    <footer>
        <p>&copy; 2024 My Application</p>
    </footer>
</body>
</html>
```

2. **Child Template**

   A child template extends the base template and fills in or overrides the defined blocks.

```html
<!-- home.html -->

{% extends "base.html" %}

{% block title %}Home{% endblock %}

{% block content %}

    <h2>Welcome to My Application</h2>

    <p>This is the home page.</p>

{% endblock %}
```

3. Program file will call the template.

```python
from flask import Flask, render_template
app = Flask(__name__)
```

```python
@app.route("/home")
def home():
    return render_template("home.html")


if __name__ == "__main__":
    app.run(debug=True)
```

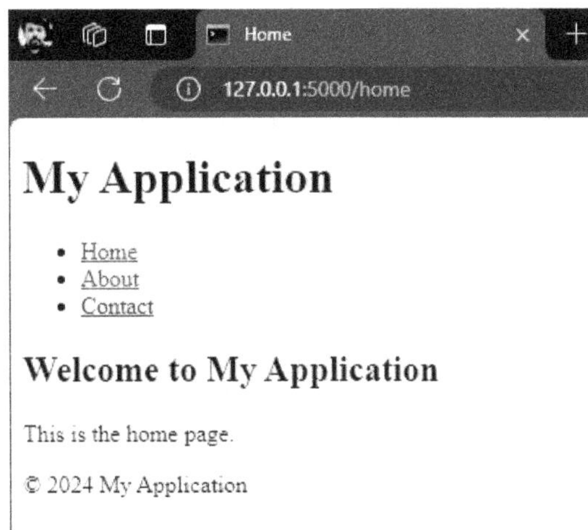


# Key Components of Template Inheritance

## 1. {% extends %}

This directive specifies the parent (base) template to inherit from. It must be the first tag in the child template.

## 2. {% block %}

Defines a block of content in the base template that child templates can override. Blocks can also have default content.

{% block block_name %}Default content{% endblock %}

## 3. Overriding Blocks

Child templates override blocks by defining them with the same name as in the base template. Content in the child template replaces the content in the base template for that block.

*Example: Multiple Child Templates*

In the example the about page modifies the title of the web page, and also added more information on the web page.

- Base Template

```
<> base01.html ✕    <> about.html    <> home01.html  ●

templates > <> base01.html > ...
     1    <!-- base01.html -->
     2    <!DOCTYPE html>
     3    <html>
     4    <head>
     5        <title>{% block title %}My Website{% endblock %}</title>
     6    </head>
     7    <body>
     8        <header>
     9            <h1>My Website</h1>
    10            <nav>
    11                <a href="/">Home</a>
    12                <a href="/about">About</a>
    13            </nav>
    14        </header>
    15        <main>
    16            {% block content %}{% endblock %}
    17        </main>
    18        <footer>
    19            <p>Footer information here</p>
    20        </footer>
    21    </body>
    22    </html>
    23
```

- Child Template 1: Home Page

```
<> base01.html      <> about.html      <> home01.html  ●

templates > <> home01.html > ...
     1    <!-- home01.html -->
     2    {% extends "base01.html" %}
     3
     4    {% block title %}Home - My Website{% endblock %}
     5
     6    {% block content %}
     7        <h2>Welcome to the Home Page</h2>
     8        <p>This is the main page of the site.</p>
     9    {% endblock %}
    10
```

- Child Template 2: About Page

`<> about01.html ✕`

`templates > <> about01.html > ...`

```html
1   <!-- about01.html -->
2   {% extends "base01.html" %}
3
4   {% block title %}About Us{% endblock %}
5
6   {% block content %}
7       <h2>About Us</h2>
8       <p>Learn more about our mission and team.</p>
9   {% endblock %}
10
```

`template006.py ✕`

`template006.py > ...`

```python
1   from flask import Flask, render_template
2
3   app = Flask(__name__)
4
5   @app.route("/home")
6   def home():
7       return render_template("home01.html")
8
9   @app.route("/about")
10  def about():
11      return render_template("about01.html")
12
13  if __name__ == "__main__":
14      app.run(debug=True)
15
```

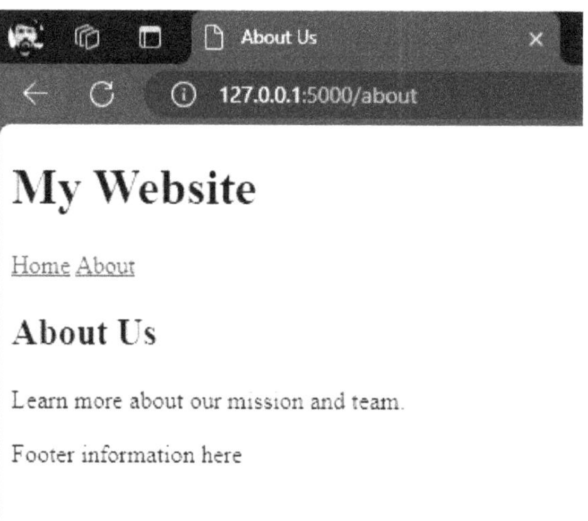

## Example Nesting Blocks

Blocks can be nested, allowing for even finer control of content inheritance.

Base Template with Nested Blocks:

In the example, below the title of the web page is being replaced by the nested home page as 'Custom title'. Also added the content from the home page, along with the content of the base template file.

- Base Template:

```
<> home02.html          <> base02.html  ×      template007.py
templates > <> base02.html > ...
    1    <!DOCTYPE html>
    2    <html>
    3    <head>
    4        <title>{% block title %}Default Title{% endblock %}</title>
    5    </head>
    6    <body>
    7        <header>
    8            {% block header %}
    9            <h1>Welcome</h1>
   10            {% endblock %}
   11        </header>
   12        <main>
   13            {% block content %}
   14            <p>Main content goes here.</p>
   15            {% endblock %}
   16        </main>
   17    </body>
   18    </html>
```

- Child Template

```html
<> home02.html  ×      <> base02.html        template007.py

templates > <> home02.html > ...
    1   {% extends "base02.html" %}
    2
    3   {% block title %}Custom Title{% endblock %}
    4
    5   {% block header %}
    6       <h1>Custom Header</h1>
    7       <p>Additional header information.</p>
    8   {% endblock %}
    9
   10   {% block content %}
   11       <p>This is custom content for the page.</p>
   12   {% endblock %}
   13
```

```python
template007.py  ×

template007.py > ...
    1   from flask import Flask, render_template
    2
    3   app = Flask(__name__)
    4
    5   @app.route("/home")
    6   def home():
    7       return render_template("home02.html")
    8
    9   if __name__ == "__main__":
   10       app.run(debug=True)
   11
```

# Best Practices for Template Inheritance

1. **Use a Clear Structure:**

   o   Store your base template as base.html or layout.html.

   o   Organize child templates in subfolders if necessary (e.g., templates/blog/post.html).

2. **Define Meaningful Block Names:**

    o   Use descriptive names like title, header, content, or sidebar for blocks.

3. **Avoid Excessive Nesting:**

    o   Keep your inheritance hierarchy simple and avoid deeply nested templates.

4. **Provide Defaults:**

    o   Always include default content in blocks to prevent errors when a block is not overridden.

5. **Reuse Components:**

    o   Break down repeated sections (e.g., headers, sidebars, footers) into their own templates and include them in the base template.

# Advantages of Template Inheritance

- **Consistency:** Ensures a uniform look and feel across all pages.

- **Code Reusability:** Reduces redundancy by centralizing common elements.

- **Maintainability:** Changes to the layout only need to be made in the base template.

Example:

- Login.html

```
Login.html
<html>
 <body>
 <form action = "http://localhost:5000/login" method = "post">
 <p>Enter Name:</p>
 <p><input type = "text" name = "nm" /></p>
 <p><input type = "submit" value = "submit" /></p>
 </form>
 </body>
</html>
```

- Loggedin.html

```
<> login.html        <> loggedin.html  ×     template008.py

templates > <> loggedin.html > ...
   1    Logedin.html
   2    <html>
   3     <body>
   4        <div>
   5            <h1>Loged in {{ name }}</h1>
   6        </div>
   7     </body>
   8    </html>
```

- Application file

```
<> login.html      <> loggedin.html      template008.py  ×

 template008.py > ...
   1    from flask import Flask, redirect, url_for, request, render_template
   2
   3    app = Flask(__name__)
   4
   5    @app.route('/')
   6    def index():
   7     return render_template('login.html')
   8
   9    @app.route('/success/<name>')
  10    def success(name):
  11        return render_template('logedin.html', name = name)
  12
  13    @app.route('/login', methods = ['POST', 'GET'])
  14    def login():
  15        if request.method == 'POST':
  16            user = request.form['nm'] + " POST"
  17            return redirect(url_for('success', name = user))
  18        else:
  19            user = request.args.get('nm') + " Get"
  20            return redirect(url_for('success', name = user))
  21
  22    if __name__ == '__main__':
  23        app.run(debug = True)
```

Moreover, **jinja2** template engine uses the following delimiters for escaping from HTML.

- {% ... %} for Statements

- {{ ... }} for Expressions to print to the template output

- {# ... #} for Comments not included in the template output

- # ... ## for Line Statements

**Example**:

In the example use of conditional statement in the template is demonstrated. The URL rule to the **check_result()** function accepts the integer parameter. It is passed to the **result.html** template. Inside the template, the value of number received (marks) is compared (greater or less than 700) and accordingly HTML is conditionally rendered.

Please note that the conditional statements **if-else** and **endif** are enclosed in delimiter **{%..%}**.

On visiting URL **http://localhost/result/700** and then **http://localhost/hello/750** to see the output of HTML changing conditionally.

```
template009.py ×     <> result.html
template009.py > ...
1    from flask import Flask, render_template
2
3    app = Flask(__name__)
4
5    @app.route('/result/<int:marks>')
6    def check_result(marks):
7        return render_template('result.html', marks = marks)
8
9    if __name__ == '__main__':
10       app.run(debug = True)
11
```

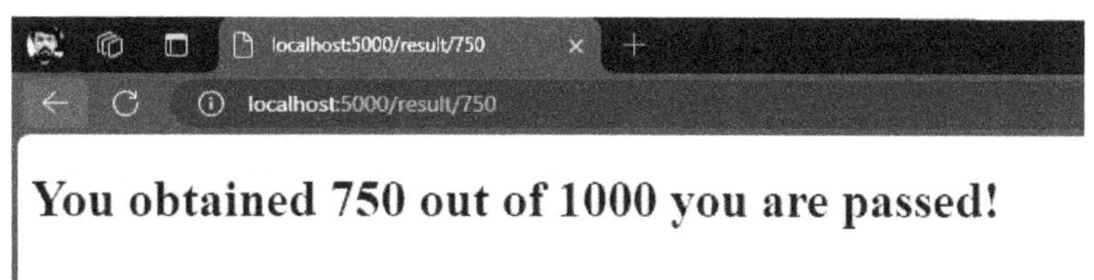

```
template009.py        result.html  ×
templates >  result.html >  html
  1   <!doctype html>
  2   <html>
  3
  4   <body>
  5       {% if marks>700 %}
  6           <h1> You obtained {{ marks }} out of 1000 you are passed!</h1>
  7       {% else %}
  8           <h1>You obtained {{ marks }} out of 1000 you are failed!</h1>
  9       {% endif %}
 10   </body>
 11
 12   </html>
```



The Template part of **result.html** employs a **for loop** to render key and value pairs of dictionary object **result{}** as cells of an HTML table.

Example:

In the example statements corresponding to the **For** loop are enclosed in {%..%} whereas, the expressions **key and value** are put inside **{{ }}**.After the development starts running, open **http://localhost:5000/result** in the browser to get the following output.

- Template File:

```
template010.py        <> marksheet.html  ×

templates > <> marksheet.html > html
    1    <!doctype html>
    2    <html>
    3
    4    <body>
    5        <table border=1>
    6            <tr>
    7                <th>Subject</th>
    8                <th>Marks</th>
    9            </tr>
   10            {% for key, value in result.items() %}
   11            <tr>
   12                <th> {{ key }} </th>
   13                <td> {{ value }} </td>
   14            </tr>
   15            {% endfor %}
   16        </table>
   17    </body>
   18
   19    </html>
```

- Application File:

```
template010.py  ×     <> marksheet.html

template010.py > ...
    1    from flask import Flask, render_template
    2
    3    app = Flask(__name__)
    4
    5    @app.route('/result')
    6    def result():
    7        marks = {'english':90,
    8                 'hindi':92,
    9                 'mathematics':98,
   10                 'physics':95,
   11                 'chemistry':96}
   12        return render_template('marksheet.html', result = marks)
   13
   14    if __name__ == '__main__':
   15        app.run(debug = True)
   16
```

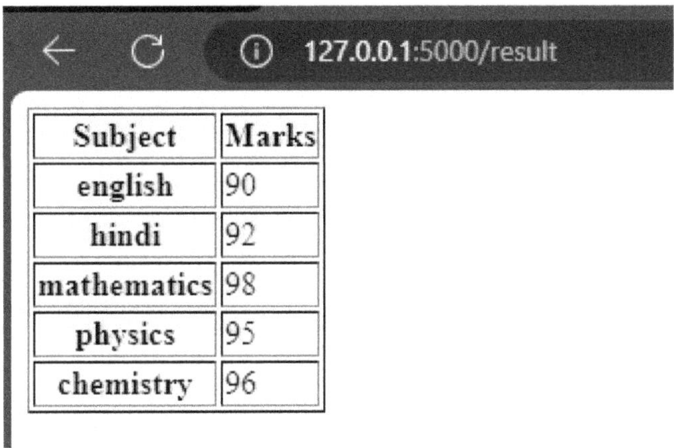


| Subject | Marks |
|---|---|
| english | 90 |
| hindi | 92 |
| mathematics | 98 |
| physics | 95 |
| chemistry | 96 |

# 10. The Static Files

Static files in Flask are files that do not change dynamically with requests or responses and are typically used for assets such as JavaScript, CSS, images, fonts, and other front-end resources. The web server is configured to serve them for you, but during the development, these files are served from *static* folder in your package or next to your module and it will be available at ***/static*** on the application. A special endpoint 'static' is used to generate URL for static files.

## What are Static Files?

- Static files are resources such as images, CSS, JavaScript, fonts, or other assets that are served as-is to the client without processing by the server.

- Flask serves these files using the static route (e.g., /static/<path-to-file>).

## Default Behaviour of Flask

- **Folder Structure**: Flask automatically looks for a folder named static in the root of application directory:

```
/project/
    app.py              # Your Flask application
    /static/            # Default static files folder
        /css/
            style.css
        /js/
            app.js
        /images/
            logo.png
```

- **URL Path**: Files in the static folder are accessible under the /static/ path. For example: /static/css/style.css

Example: Using Static Files

**CSS File (static/css/style.css):**

Style.css File:

```
static > css > # style.css > ...
1   body {
2       background-color: #a4eed2;
3       font-family: Arial, sans-serif;
4   }
5
```

Index.html File:

```
static001.py       # style.css        <> index.html  ×

templates > <> index.html > ...
  1   <!-- index.html -->
  2   <!DOCTYPE html>
  3   <html lang="en">
  4   <head>
  5       <link rel="stylesheet" href="{{ url_for('static', filename='css/style.css') }}">
  6       <title>Static Files Example</title>
  7   </head>
  8   <body>
  9       <h1>Welcome to Flask!</h1>
 10   </body>
 11   </html>
```

Application File:

```
static001.py  ×    # style.css        <> index.html

static001.py > ...
  1     from flask import Flask, render_template
  2
  3     app = Flask(__name__)
  4
  5     @app.route('/')
  6     def index():
  7         return render_template('index.html')
  8
  9     if __name__ == '__main__':
 10         app.run(debug = True)
 11
```

Look at the colour of the background of the page.

# Customizing the Static Folder

- By default, Flask uses a folder named static. You can change this default behaviour by specifying a custom folder name: `app = Flask(__name__, static_folder='assets')`

- Example folder structure:

```
/project/
    app.py
    /assets/
        main.css
```

- The files will then be accessible at /static/<filename>: /static/main.css

# Organizing Static Files

To maintain a clean project structure, organize files into subdirectories:

- /static/css/: For stylesheets.

- /static/js/: For JavaScript files.

- /static/images/: For image assets.

- /static/fonts/: For fonts.

Example:

Folder Structure:

```
/static/
    /css/
        style.css
    /js/
        script.js
    /images/
        logo.png
```

HTML Template:

```html
<link rel="stylesheet" href="{{ url_for('static', filename='css/style.css') }}">
<script src="{{ url_for('static', filename='js/script.js') }}"></script>
<img src="{{ url_for('static', filename='images/logo.png') }}" alt="Logo">
```

# Working with Blueprints

- Blueprints in Flask can define their own static folders. This is useful when your app is modularized.

```python
# static002.py
from flask import Flask
from flask import Blueprint

app = Flask(__name__)

admin_bp = Blueprint('admin', __name__, static_folder='admin_static')

# Register blueprint
app.register_blueprint(admin_bp, url_prefix='/admin')

if __name__ == '__main__':
    app.run(debug = True)
```

Static files can now be accessed using the URL: /admin/static/<filename>

# Cache Busting

Browsers often cache static files, so changes may not appear immediately. To prevent this, use cache-busting techniques like appending a version or timestamp to the file URL:

```html
<link rel="stylesheet" href="{{ url_for('static', filename='css/style.css', v='1.0') }}">
<!-- OR -->
<link rel="stylesheet" href="{{ url_for('static', filename='css/style.css') }}?v={{ time.time() }}">
```

Example:

Script File:

```javascript
function sayHelloWorld() {
    alert("Hello World!")
}
```

Template File:

```html
<!doctype html>
<html>

<head>
    <script type="text/javascript" src="{{ url_for('static', filename = 'helloworld.js') }}"></script>
</head>

<body>
    <input type = "button" onclick = "sayHelloWorld()" value = "Say Hello World!" />
</body>

</html>
```

Application File:

```python
from flask import Flask, render_template

app = Flask(__name__)

@app.route('/')
def index():
    return render_template('static02.html')

if __name__ == '__main__':
    app.run(debug = True)
```

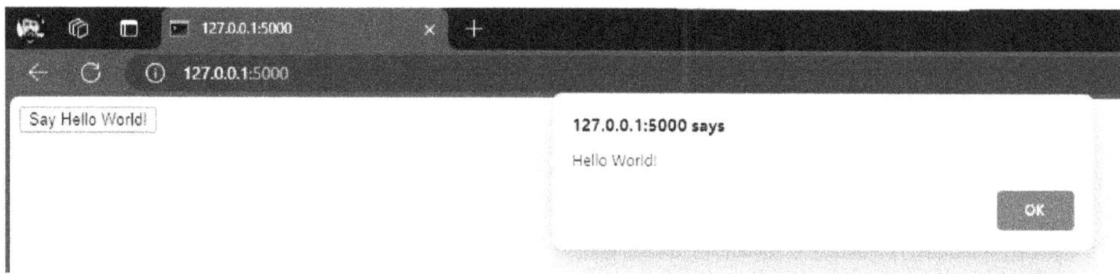

On inspecting in the web browser.

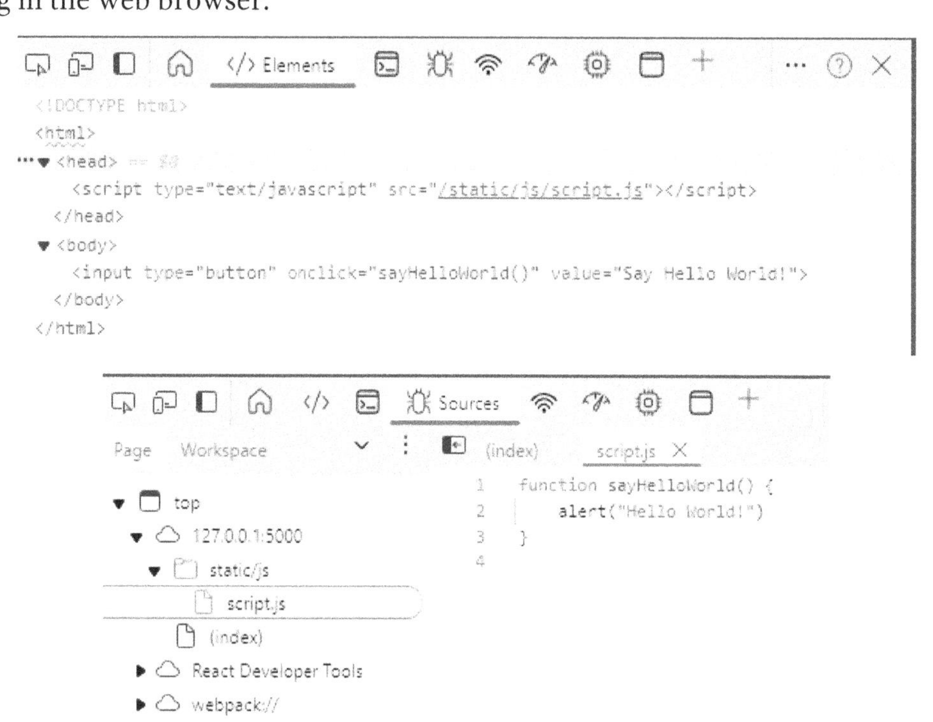

# 11. Accessing Request Data

## The Request Object

A **request object** in Flask, used to access data sent by the client to a Flask application. This object is provided by the Flask framework and imported from flask. The data from a client web page is sent to the server as a global request object. To process the request data, it should be imported from the Flask module.

Importing the request Object:

from flask import Flask, request

Key Attributes of the request Object

1. request.method

   o   The HTTP method used for the request (e.g., GET, POST, PUT, DELETE).

```python
if request.method == 'POST':
    print("This is a POST request.")
```

2. request.args

   o   A MultiDict containing the parsed query string (URL parameters).

   o   Useful for GET parameters (?key=value in URLs).

```python
name = request.args.get('name')   # Access ?name=Somnath
```

3. request.form

   o   A MultiDict containing form data from POST or PUT requests.

```python
email = request.form['email']
```

4. request.data

   o   Raw binary data from the request body.

   o   Useful for handling non-form or non-JSON payloads. raw_data = request.data

5. request.json

   o   Parsed JSON data from the request body.

```python
json_data = request.json
```

6. request.headers

   o   A dictionary-like object containing HTTP headers.

```python
user_agent = request.headers.get('User-Agent')
```

7. request.cookies

- o A dictionary of cookies sent by the client.

```python
session_id = request.cookies.get('session_id')
```

8. request.files

- o A MultiDict of uploaded files (if any).

```python
uploaded_file = request.files['file']
```

9. request.remote_addr

- o The IP address of the client.

```python
client_ip = request.remote_addr
```

10. request.url

- o The full URL requested by the client.

```python
full_url = request.url
```

11. request.path

- o The URL path portion of the request.

```python
path = request.path
```

12. request.endpoint

- o The endpoint of the current request.

```python
endpoint = request.endpoint
```

13. request.view_args

- o A dictionary of arguments captured from the URL route.

```python
@app.route('/user/<username>')
def user_profile(username):
    print(request.view_args['username'])  # Outputs the captured username
```

# Common Use Cases

### 1. Handling Query Parameters (GET)

```python
@app.route('/search')
def search():
    query = request.args.get('q', '')  # Default to an empty string
    return f"Search query: {query}"
```

### 2. Handling Form Data (POST)

```python
@app.route('/submit', methods=['POST'])
def submit_form():
    username = request.form.get('username')
    return f"Hello, {username}!"
```

### 3. Handling JSON Payload

```python
@app.route('/api/data', methods=['POST'])
def api_data():
    data = request.json
    return f"Received: {data}"
```

### 4. Uploading Files

```python
@app.route('/upload', methods=['POST'])
def upload_file():
    if 'file' not in request.files:
        return "No file uploaded!"
    file = request.files['file']
    file.save(f"./uploads/{file.filename}")
    return "File uploaded successfully!"
```

### 5. Accessing HTTP Headers

```python
@app.route('/')
def home():
    user_agent = request.headers.get('User-Agent')
    return f"Your user agent: {user_agent}"
```

6.

Debugging and Introspection

- Use request.__dict__ to explore all attributes and methods of the request object during runtime.

```python
print(request.__dict__)
```

# Example: Handling a User Registration Form

In this example, a Flask route handles a user registration form. The form sends data via POST, including query parameters, form data, and files.

**App.py**

```python
from flask import Flask, request, render_template


app = Flask(__name__)
```

```python
@app.route('/')
def index():
    return render_template('register.html')


@app.route('/register', methods=['GET', 'POST'])
def register():
    if request.method == 'GET':
        # Handle query parameters (e.g., /register?ref=google)
        referrer = request.args.get('ref', 'direct')
        return f"Registration page referred by: {referrer}"


    if request.method == 'POST':
        # Handle form data
        username = request.form.get('username')
        email = request.form.get('email')

        # Handle file upload
        profile_pic = request.files.get('profile_pic')
        if profile_pic:
            file_path = f"./uploads/{profile_pic.filename}"
            profile_pic.save(file_path)
        else:
            file_path = "No profile picture uploaded"

        # Handle JSON payload (optional)
        additional_data = request.json if request.is_json else None

        # Client info
        client_ip = request.remote_addr
        user_agent = request.headers.get('User-Agent')

        return f"""
        Registration Successful!<br>
        Username: {username}<br>
        Email: {email}<br>
        Profile Picture Saved: {file_path}<br>
        Additional Data: {additional_data}<br>
        Client IP: {client_ip}<br>
        User Agent: {user_agent}
        """
```

```python
if __name__ == '__main__':
    app.run(debug=True)
```

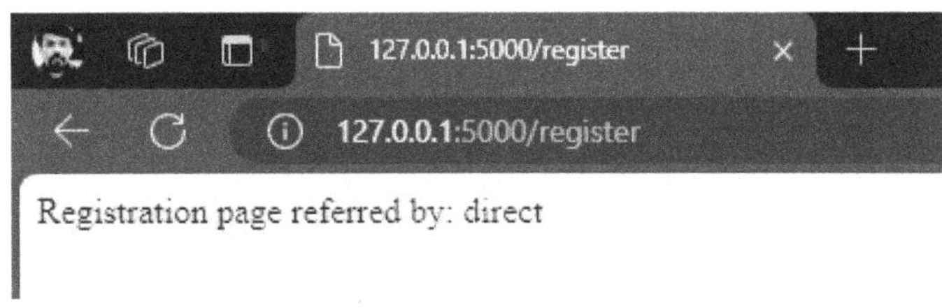


## How it Works:

1. **GET Request**: Displays the referrer from query parameters (e.g., ?ref=google).

2. **POST Request**: Handles:

    o   Form data (e.g., username and email).

    o   File uploads (e.g., profile_pic).

    o   JSON payloads (if sent with Content-Type: application/json).

    o   Client metadata (e.g., IP address and User-Agent).

## Testing the Example:

- **GET Request:**

    Open /register?ref=google in a browser.

- **POST Request:**

    Use a tool like **Postman** or a custom HTML form:

```html
<> register.html  ×

templates > <> register.html > ...
    1   <form action="/register" method="POST" enctype="multipart/form-data">
    2       <input type="text" name="username" placeholder="Username"><br>
    3       <input type="email" name="email" placeholder="Email"><br>
    4       <input type="file" name="profile_pic"><br>
    5       <button type="submit">Register</button>
    6   </form>
    7
```

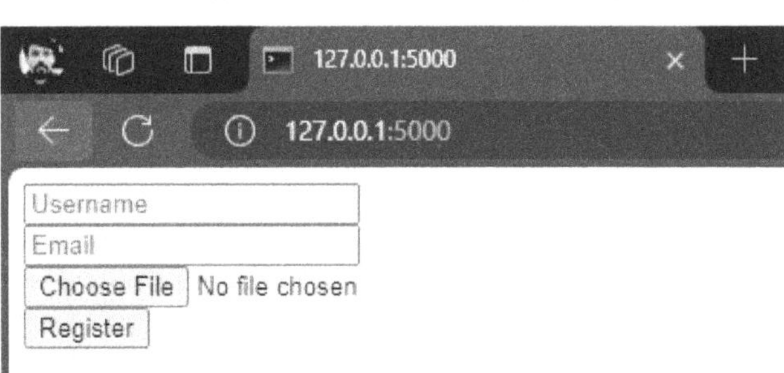

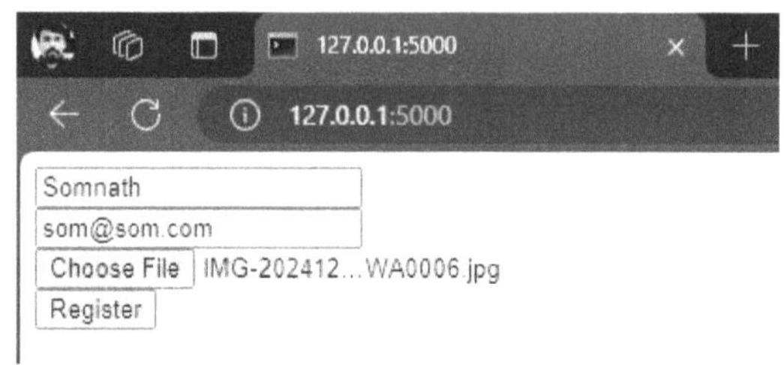

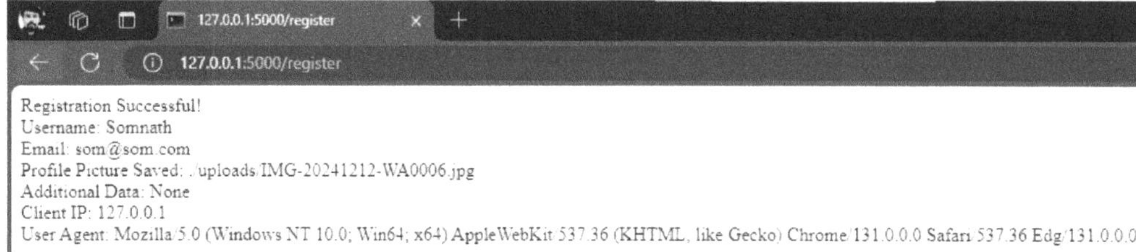

# Sending Form Data to Template

### Overview

Sending form data to a template in Flask involves three main steps:

1. **Creating an HTML form** to capture user input.

2. **Handling form submission** in a Flask route.

3. **Passing the form data** to a template for rendering.

The HTTP method can be specified in the URL rule, as we have seen earlier. The form data received by the triggered function is collected as a dictionary object, which can then be passed to a template for rendering on the corresponding web page.

Example Project Directory Structure:

```
project/
|
├── app.py              # Flask application file
├── templates/
|    ├── form.html       # HTML form
|    └── success.html    # Success page
└── static/
     └── (optional for CSS/JS files)
```

# Creating an HTML Form

HTML forms are used to collect user input. Key components:

- The method attribute (usually POST for sending data securely).

- The action attribute specifies where the form data should be submitted (a route in your Flask app).

- Input fields to capture user data.

Template File:

```html
<form method="POST" action="/submit_form">
    <label for="username">Username:</label>
    <input type="text" id="username" name="username" required>

    <label for="email">Email:</label>
    <input type="email" id="email" name="email" required>

    <button type="submit">Submit</button>
</form>
```

## Handling Form Submission in Flask

In Flask, use routes to handle form submissions. Use request.form to access form data.

Application File

```python
from flask import Flask, request, render_template

app = Flask(__name__)

@app.route('/')
def home():
    return render_template('form.html')  # Display the form

@app.route('/submit_form', methods=['POST'])
def submit_form():
    # Extract data from the form
    username = request.form.get('username')  # Retrieve 'username' field
    email = request.form.get('email')  # Retrieve 'email' field

    # Pass the form data to a template
    return render_template('success.html', username=username, email=email)

if __name__ == '__main__':
    app.run(debug=True)
```

Explanation:

- request.form: A dictionary-like object to access form fields by their name attribute.

- render_template: Renders an HTML file and passes variables to it.

# Passing Data to the Template

Data is passed to the template via render_template. Use placeholders in the template to display the data.

```
<> form.html          robj003.py          <> success.html  ×

templates > <> success.html > ...
    1    <!DOCTYPE html>
    2    <html lang="en">
    3    <head>
    4        <meta charset="UTF-8">
    5        <meta name="viewport" content="width=device-width, initial-scale=1.0">
    6        <title>Form Submission</title>
    7    </head>
    8    <body>
    9        <h1>Form Submitted Successfully!</h1>
   10        <p>Welcome, {{ username }}!</p>
   11        <p>Your email is {{ email }}.</p>
   12    </body>
   13    </html>
```

Flask Variables in Templates:

{{ username }} and {{ email }} are placeholders replaced by the passed values.

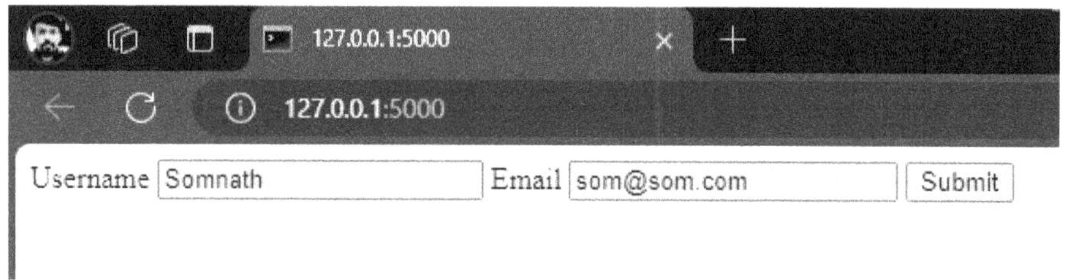


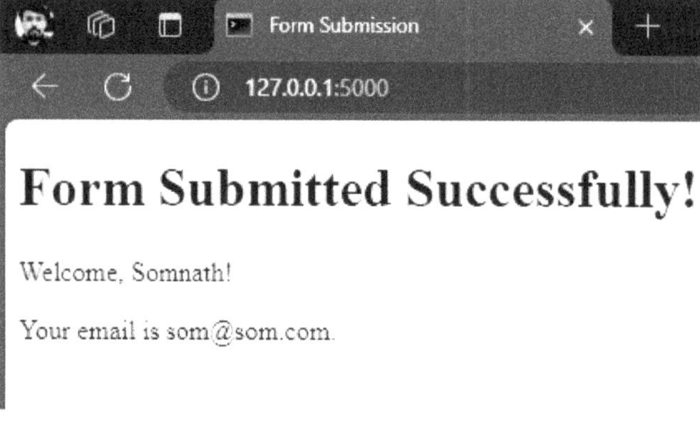


# CSRF Protection

For security, include CSRF protection when dealing with forms. Use the Flask-WTF extension.

Setup CSRF with Flask-WTF: pip install flask-wtf

Application File:

```python
from flask import Flask, render_template, request
from flask_wtf import FlaskForm
from wtforms import StringField, EmailField, SubmitField
from wtforms.validators import DataRequired
from flask_wtf.csrf import CSRFProtect

app = Flask(__name__)
app.secret_key = 'your_secret_key'
csrf = CSRFProtect(app)

class MyForm(FlaskForm):
    username = StringField('Username', validators=[DataRequired()])
    email = EmailField('Email', validators=[DataRequired()])
    submit = SubmitField('Submit')

@app.route('/', methods=['GET', 'POST'])
def form():
    form = MyForm()
    if form.validate_on_submit():
        username = form.username.data
        email = form.email.data
        return render_template('success.html', username=username, email=email)
    return render_template('form01.html', form=form)

if __name__ == '__main__':
    app.run(debug=True)
```

Template File:

```html
<form method="POST">
    {{ form.hidden_tag() }}
    {{ form.username.label }} {{ form.username }}
    {{ form.email.label }} {{ form.email }}
    {{ form.submit }}
</form>
```

The result will be same as in the earlier example. Flask -WTF is discussed in detail in the later part of the book

Best Practices

1. **Validation**: Always validate form inputs server-side (and optionally client-side for user experience).

2. **Error Handling**: Display error messages for invalid inputs.

3. **Sanitize Inputs**: Use frameworks' built-in mechanisms to avoid XSS and SQL injection.

4. **Use CSRF Tokens**: Protect against CSRF attacks when handling forms.

# 12. The Cookies

Cookies are a mechanism used to store data on the client side, allowing web applications to retain user information between requests. In Flask, cookies are managed through the request and response objects. A cookie is a small text file stored on a client's computer. Its primary purpose is to remember and track data related to the client's usage, enhancing the user experience and providing site statistics.

In Flask, cookies are managed through the Request and Response objects. The Request object contains a dictionary of all transmitted cookies and their corresponding values, accessible via request.cookies. A cookie also includes additional attributes like expiry time, path, and the domain name of the site.

To set a cookie in Flask, use the make_response() function to create a response object from a view function's return value. Then, call the set_cookie() method on the response object to store the cookie.

Reading a cookie is straightforward; you can use the get() method on the request.cookies attribute to retrieving a specific cookie's value.

## How Cookies Work

1. **Setting a Cookie:** The server sends a Set-Cookie header in the HTTP response.

2. **Storing a Cookie:** The client (browser) stores the cookie and sends it back to the server in subsequent requests using the Cookie header.

3. **Accessing a Cookie:** The server reads the cookie from the Cookie header to retrieve information about the user.

## Cookies in Flask

Flask provides easy-to-use methods to set, access, and delete cookies. Below are the key methods and concepts:

**Setting a Cookie**

To set a cookie in Flask, you use the set_cookie method of the response object.

```python
from flask import Flask, make_response

app = Flask(__name__)

@app.route('/set_cookie')
def set_cookie():
    resp = make_response("Cookie is set")
    resp.set_cookie('username', 'JohnDoe')  # Key-value pair
    return resp
```

**Parameters of set_cookie:**

- key: Name of the cookie (e.g., 'username').

- value: Value of the cookie (e.g., 'JohnDoe').

- max_age: Duration in seconds before the cookie expires.

- expires: Specific expiration date and time.

- path: Path where the cookie is valid.

- secure: Ensures the cookie is sent only over HTTPS.

- httponly: Restricts access to cookies from client-side scripts.

### Accessing a Cookie

You can access cookies from the request object.

```python
@app.route('/get_cookie')
def get_cookie():
    username = request.cookies.get('username')  # Returns None if cookie does not exist
    return f"Username: {username}"
```

### Deleting a Cookie

To delete a cookie, use the set_cookie method with an empty value and an immediate expiration time.

```python
@app.route('/delete_cookie')
def delete_cookie():
    resp = make_response("Cookie is deleted")
    resp.set_cookie('username', '', expires=0)
    return resp
```

### Best Practices for Using Cookies in Flask

1. **Secure Sensitive Information:** Never store sensitive data like passwords directly in cookies. Use cryptographic tools like Flask's itsdangerous module to securely sign cookies.

2. **Use secure Flag:** Always use the secure flag for cookies in production to prevent them from being sent over non-HTTPS connections.

3. **HttpOnly:** Enable the httponly flag to prevent cookies from being accessed by client-side scripts.

4. **Limit Scope:** Use the path parameter to limit the scope of cookies to specific parts of the application.

5. **Consider SameSite:** Use the SameSite attribute to protect against Cross-Site Request Forgery (CSRF) attacks.

```python
resp.set_cookie('username', 'JohnDoe', samesite='Strict')
```

### Use Case Example

Below is a full example demonstrating setting, accessing, and deleting cookies in a Flask application.

```python
from flask import Flask, request, make_response

app = Flask(__name__)

@app.route('/set')
def set_cookie():
    resp = make_response("Cookie set!")
    resp.set_cookie('framework', 'Flask', max_age=60*60*24)  # Expires in 1 day
    return resp

@app.route('/get')
def get_cookie():
    framework = request.cookies.get('framework')
    if framework:
        return f"Framework: {framework}"
    return "No cookie found!"

@app.route('/delete')
def delete_cookie():
    resp = make_response("Cookie deleted!")
    resp.set_cookie('framework', '', expires=0)
    return resp

if __name__ == '__main__':
    app.run(debug=True)
```

# Common Issues and Debugging

1. **Cookies Not Persisting:** Ensure the browser accepts cookies and the domain and path parameters match your application setup.

2. **Cross-Domain Issues:** Use CORS settings and proper cookie attributes (samesite, secure, etc.) for cross-origin applications.

3. **Size Limitations:** Keep cookies small; most browsers limit total cookie size to about 4KB.

# Just an Example:

Template File:

```
cookie003.py        <> readcookie.html  ×
templates > <> readcookie.html > ...
    1    <!-- readcookie.html -->
    2    <h5>
    3        Cookie UserId is set
    4    </h5>
    5    <hr>
    6    <a href="getcookie">Click here to read the cookie.</a>
    7
```

```
<> login.html  ×
templates > <> login.html > @ html
    1    <html>
    2
    3    <body>
    4        <form action="http://localhost:5000/login" method="post">
    5            <p>Enter Name:</p>
    6            <p><input type="text" name="nm" /></p>
    7            <p><input type="submit" value="submit" /></p>
    8        </form>
    9    </body>
    10
    11    </html>
```

Application File:

cookie003.py ✕ <> readcookie.html

cookie003.py > ...

```python
from flask import Flask, request, make_response, render_template

app = Flask(__name__)

@app.route('/')
def index():
    return render_template('login.html')

@app.route('/login', methods = ['POST', 'GET'])
def setcookie():
    if request.method == 'POST':
        user = request.form['nm']
        resp = make_response(render_template('readcookie.html'))
        resp.set_cookie('userID', user)
        return resp

@app.route('/getcookie')
def getcookie():
    name = request.cookies.get('userID')
    return '<h1>welcome '+name+'</h1>'

if __name__ == '__main__':
    app.run()
```

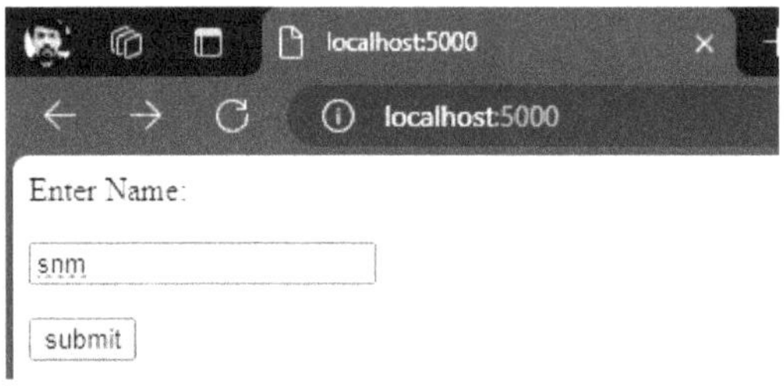

# 13. The Sessions

**Session** in Flask is a mechanism that allows you to store information across multiple requests from the same user. It provides a way to maintain user data between requests by storing it server-side and associating it with a specific client via cookies

Like cookies, session data is stored on the client side. A session refers to the period between when a client logs into a server and logs out. Any data that needs to persist throughout this session is stored in the client's browser.

Each session is assigned a unique Session ID. Session data is stored on top of cookies and is cryptographically signed by the server. To enable this encryption, a Flask application requires a defined SECRET_KEY.

The session object is essentially a dictionary that holds key-value pairs of session variables and their corresponding values. For example, to set a 'username' session variable, you can use the following statement:

session['username'] = 'admin'

To remove a session variable, the pop() method is used:

session.pop('username', None)

Why Use Sessions?

HTTP is a stateless protocol, meaning that the server does not retain any information about the user's state between requests. Sessions solve this problem by storing user-specific data that persists across multiple interactions. Common use cases include:

- User authentication (e.g., tracking logged-in users)

- Storing preferences or settings

- Shopping cart data in e-commerce applications

How Flask Sessions Work?

Flask sessions use a cryptographically signed cookie to store session data on the client-side. This ensures that the data cannot be tampered with without detection.

- The session data is serialized using **secure cookies** (implemented by *itsdangerous* library).

- A secret key is used to sign the cookie, ensuring data integrity.

- Flask does not store session data on the server; it is stored in the cookie sent to the client.

**Setting Up Sessions in Flask**

To use sessions, you need to configure a secret key in your Flask app. This key is used to sign the session data.

```python
session001.py > ...
1    from flask import Flask, session
2
3    app = Flask(__name__)
4
5    # Set a secret key for securing sessions
6    app.secret_key = 'your_secret_key_here'
7
```

## Using Flask Sessions

- **Storing Data in the Session**

    o You can store data in the session like a Python dictionary.

    ```python
    6    @app.route('/set_session')
    7    def set_session():
    8        session['username'] = 'JohnDoe'
    9        return "Session data set!"
    ```

- **Accessing Data from the Session**

    o You can retrieve data from the session similarly.

    ```python
    11    @app.route('/get_session')
    12    def get_session():
    13        username = session.get('username', 'Guest')
    14        return f"Hello, {username}!"
    ```
    o

- **Removing Data from the Session**

    o You can remove specific session data using the pop method or clear the entire session.

    ```python
    16    # Remove a specific key
    17    @app.route('/remove_session')
    18    def remove_session():
    19        session.pop('username', None)
    20        return "Removed"
    21
    22    # Clear the entire session
    23    @app.route('/remove_entire_session')
    24    def remove_entire_session():
    25        session.clear()
    26        return "Removed Entire"
    27
    ```

- **Security Considerations:**

- o **Secret Key**: Always set a strong, random secret key and keep it private.

- o **HTTPS**: Use HTTPS to prevent session cookies from being intercepted.

- o **Secure Cookie**: Set the SESSION_COOKIE_SECURE option to True to ensure cookies are only sent over HTTPS.

- o **Session Expiry**: Configure session lifetime to limit how long a session remains active.

```python
# Example of setting session lifetime (default is permanent session)
from datetime import timedelta

app.permanent_session_lifetime = timedelta(minutes=30)
```

- **Configuration Options for Sessions**

  - o Flask provides several configuration options to control session behaviour:

| Option | Description |
| --- | --- |
| SECRET_KEY | A key used to encrypt the session data. |
| SESSION_COOKIE_NAME | The name of the session cookie. Default is session. |
| SESSION_COOKIE_SECURE | Ensures cookies are sent only over HTTPS. |
| SESSION_COOKIE_HTTPONLY | Prevents JavaScript from accessing the session cookie. Default is True. |
| SESSION_COOKIE_SAMESITE | Limits cross-site cookie usage. Values: 'Lax' (default) or 'Strict'. |
| PERMANENT_SESSION_LIFETIME | The lifetime of a permanent session. Default is 31 days. |

- **Advantages of Flask Sessions**

  - o **Ease of Use**: Simple dictionary-like interface.

  - o **Client-Side Storage**: Eliminates the need for server-side storage for small amounts of data.

  - o **Integrity**: Secure signing prevents tampering.

- **Limitations**

  - o **Client-Side Storage:** Limited to what can fit in a cookie (generally 4KB).

  - o **Not for Sensitive Data:** Avoid storing sensitive information like passwords.

  - o **Dependent on Cookies:** Users must have cookies enabled for sessions to work.

- **Extending Flask Sessions**

- o For larger or more secure data storage, you can use server-side session extensions like Flask-Session. This allows session data to be stored in a database, Redis, or filesystem instead of cookies.

# Example:

Session.py File:

```python
from flask import Flask, session, request, redirect, url_for
app = Flask(__name__)
app.secret_key = 'some secred key'


@app.route('/')
def index():
    if 'userid' in session:
        userid = session['userid']
        return '<h2>You are Logged in as ' + userid + '</h2><br>' + \
                "<b><a href = '/logout'>You can click here to log out.</a></b>"
    return "<h2>You are not logged in.<h2><br><a href = '/login'></b>" + \
            "Click here to log in</b></a>"


@app.route('/login', methods = ['GET', 'POST'])
def login():
    if request.method == 'POST':
        session['userid'] = request.form['userid']
        return redirect(url_for('index'))
    return '''
            <form action = "" method = "post">
            <p><input type = "text" name = "userid"/></p>
            <p><input type = "submit" value = "Login"/></p>
            </form>
            '''


@app.route('/logout')
def logout():
    # remove the username from the session if it is there
    session.pop('userid', None)
    return redirect(url_for('index'))


if __name__ == '__main__':
    app.run(debug = True)
```

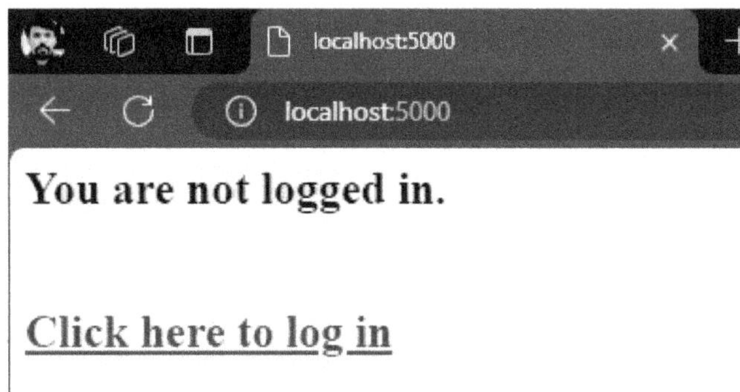
localhost:5000
localhost:5000
You are not logged in.
Click here to log in

localhost:5000/login
localhost:5000/login
Somnath
Login

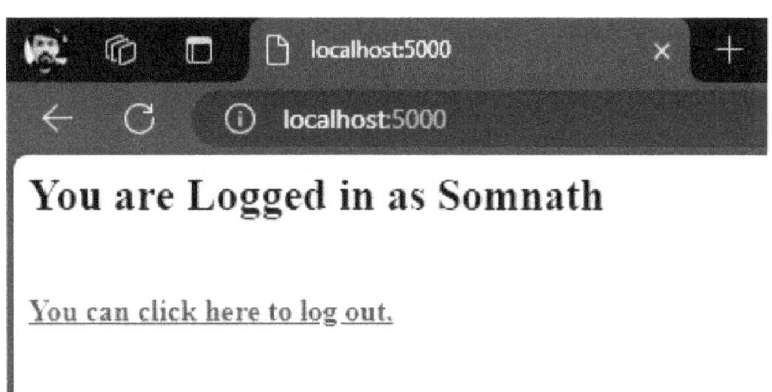
localhost:5000
localhost:5000
You are Logged in as Somnath
You can click here to log out.

# 14. Redirect & Errors

As Flask is a micro web framework in Python that allows developers to handle web requests and responses efficiently. Two essential aspects of web development with Flask are redirects and error handling.

## Redirects in Flask

A redirect in Flask is used to send a user to a different endpoint or URL. This is commonly used in scenarios like user authentication, form submissions, or URL restructuring.

**Key Points about Redirects:**

1. **HTTP Status Code**: A redirect typically uses HTTP status codes like:

   - 302 Found (default): Temporary redirection.

   - 301 Moved Permanently: For permanent URL changes.

   - 307 Temporary Redirect or 308 Permanent Redirect: Retains the HTTP method (e.g., POST remains POST).

2. **Implementation in Flask**:

   - Flask provides a simple function, redirect(), to implement redirections. You can pair this with url_for() to dynamically generate URLs.

## Example of Redirect:

```python
from flask import Flask, redirect, url_for

app = Flask(__name__)

@app.route('/')
def home():
    return "Welcome to the Home Page!"

@app.route('/old-page')
def old_page():
    # Redirecting to the new page
    return redirect(url_for('new_page'))

@app.route('/new-page')
def new_page():
    return "Welcome to the New Page!"

if __name__ == '__main__':
    app.run(debug=True)
```

On visiting the page: http://127.0.0.1:5000/old-page

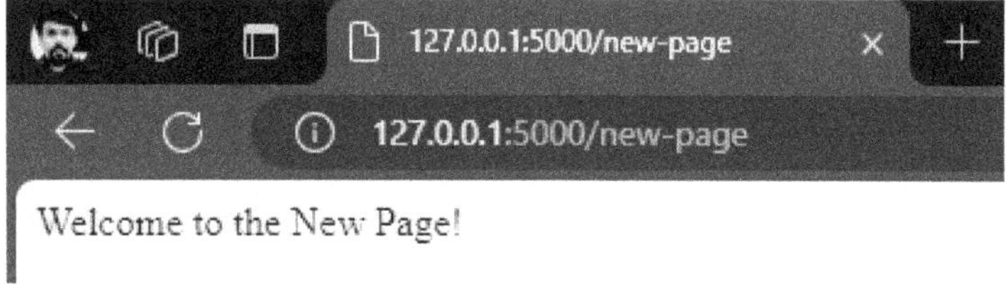


**Use Cases:**

- Redirecting to a login page if a user is not authenticated.

- Forwarding users to a thank-you page after form submission.

- Permanently moving deprecated endpoints to new URLs.

# Error Handling in Flask

Flask includes mechanisms to manage errors and return custom responses when things go wrong. This ensures a smooth user experience and helps developers debug issues efficiently.

**Common HTTP Errors:**

1. **400 Bad Request**: Malformed or invalid client request.

2. **403 Forbidden**: Access denied to a resource.

3. **404 Not Found**: Requested resource does not exist.

4. **500 Internal Server Error**: General server-side error.

**Handling Errors in Flask:**

Flask provides the @app.errorhandler decorator to define custom behaviour for specific errors.

**Example of Error Handling:**

```
redirect002.py ×
redirect002.py > ...
 6    def home():
 7        return "Welcome to the Home Page!"
 8
 9    @app.route('/error')
10    def trigger_error():
11        # Simulating an error
12        raise ValueError("This is a simulated error!")
13
14    @app.errorhandler(404)
15    def handle_404_error(error):
16        return "Oops! Page not found. Please check the URL.", 404
17
18    @app.errorhandler(500)
19    def handle_500_error(error):
20        return f"Server Error: {error}", 500
21
22    if __name__ == '__main__':
23        app.run(debug=True)
```

**Custom Error Pages:**

You can also render custom templates for errors to enhance user experience:

```
@app.errorhandler(404)
def handle_404_error(error):
    return render_template('404.html'), 404
```

**Use Cases:**

- Displaying user-friendly error pages.

- Logging detailed error information for debugging.

- Safeguarding sensitive error details by not exposing them to the user.

**Best Practices for Redirects and Errors:**

1. **Use url_for()**: Always use url_for() with redirect() to avoid hardcoding URLs.

2. **Define Custom Error Pages**: Ensure every common HTTP error has a meaningful response or page.

3. **Log Errors**: Use Flask extensions like Flask-Logging to record error details.

4. **Test Error Scenarios**: Validate custom error handlers and redirects during development.

By mastering redirects and error handling, you can create more intuitive and resilient web applications with Flask.

Some of status codes are standard:

- HTTP_300_MULTIPLE_CHOICES

- HTTP_301_MOVED_PERMANENTLY

- HTTP_302_FOUND

- HTTP_303_SEE_OTHER

- HTTP_304_NOT_MODIFIED

- HTTP_305_USE_PROXY

- HTTP_306_RESERVED

- HTTP_307_TEMPORARY_REDIRECT

The **default status** code is **302**, which is for **'found'**.

The **Code** parameter takes one of following values –

- **400** – for Bad Request

- **401** – for Unauthenticated

- **403** – for Forbidden

- **404** – for Not Found

- **406** – for Not Acceptable

- **415** – for Unsupported Media Type

- **429** – Too Many Requests

# Example:

Application File:

```
redirect003.py  ×

redirect003.py > ...
1   from flask import Flask, redirect, url_for, render_template, request
2
3   app = Flask(__name__)
4
5   @app.route('/')
6   def index():
7       return render_template('login.html')
8
9   @app.route('/login',methods = ['POST', 'GET'])
10  def login():
11      if request.method == 'POST' and request.form['nm'] == 'admin' :
12          return redirect(url_for('success'))
13      else:
14          return redirect(url_for('index'))
15
16  @app.route('/success')
17  def success():
18      return 'logged in successfully'
19
20  if __name__ == '__main__':
21      app.run(debug = True)
```

login.html

```
redirect003.py        <> login.html  ×

templates > <> login.html > ...
1    <html>
2
3    <body>
4        <form action="http://localhost:5000/login" method="post">
5            <p>Enter Name:</p>
6            <p><input type="text" name="nm" /></p>
7            <p><input type="submit" value="submit" /></p>
8        </form>
9    </body>
10
11   </html>
```

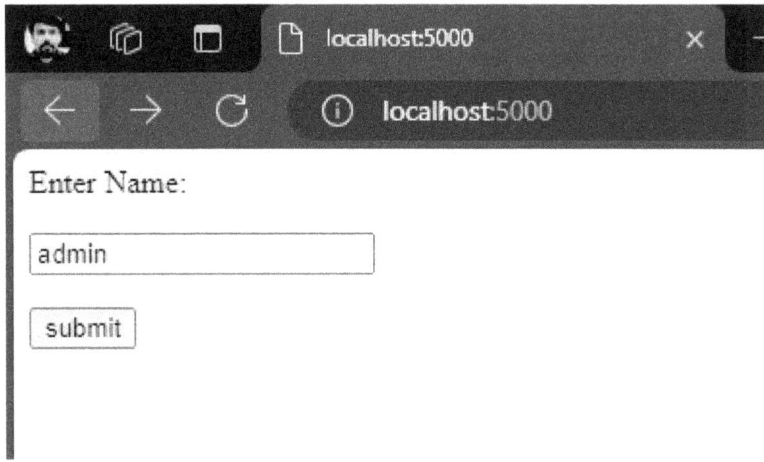



If we modify the Application File:

```
redirect004.py
redirect004.py > ...
1   from flask import Flask, redirect, url_for, render_template, request, abort
2   app = Flask(__name__)
3
4   @app.route('/')
5   def index():
6       return render_template('login.html')
7
8   @app.route('/login',methods = ['POST', 'GET'])
9   def login():
10      if request.method == 'POST':
11          if request.form['nm'] == 'admin' :
12              return redirect(url_for('success'))
13          else:
14              abort(401)
15      else:
16          return redirect(url_for('index'))
17
18  @app.route('/success')
19  def success():
20      return 'logged in successfully'
21
22  if __name__ == '__main__':
23      app.run(debug = True)
24
```

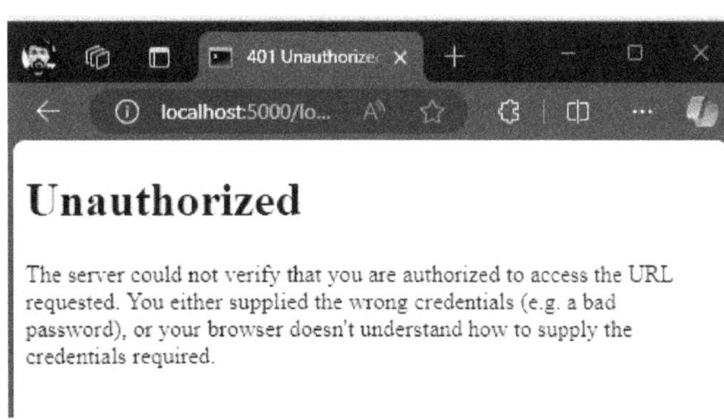

# 15. Message Flashing

## What is Message Flashing?

Message flashing is a way for the server to temporarily store and display one-time messages to users. These messages are often used to convey feedback, status updates, or notifications. For instance:

- Informing users about the success or failure of an operation.

- Displaying login or logout notifications.

- Providing system alerts, such as "Feature not available."

Flashing ensures messages persist through redirects, making it ideal for workflows like form submissions or multi-step processes.

An effective GUI-based application offers feedback to users about their interactions. For instance, desktop applications use dialog or message boxes, while JavaScript often employs alerts for this purpose.

In Flask web applications, generating such informative messages is straightforward. The framework's flashing system enables the creation of messages in one view, which can then be displayed in a subsequent view function.

## Core Concepts

1. **Temporary Storage:**

   Flash messages are stored in Flask's session for a single request-response cycle. Once accessed using get_flashed_messages(), they are removed.

2. **Session Dependency:**

   Flashing relies on sessions, so your Flask app must have a secret_key defined. This key is essential for securely signing session cookies.

3. **Message Categories:**

   Categories help group messages by type (e.g., "success", "error"). Categories allow for customized behaviour and styling.

## Key Functions

1. **flash(message, category=None)**

   o   Stores a message in the session.

   o   Optionally accepts a category to classify the message (e.g., "success", "error").

- o Default category is "message" if none is provided.

```
flash("Your changes have been saved.", "success")
```

2. **get_flashed_messages(with_categories=False, category_filter=[])**

- Retrieves and clears all flashed messages.

- Parameters:

    - o with_categories: If True, returns a list of (category, message) tuples.

    - o category_filter: Filters messages by specific categories.

```
messages = get_flashed_messages(with_categories=True, category_filter=["error", "info"])
```

Step-by-Step Setup

**A. Basic Flask App with Flash Messages:**

**a. Setup Flask App and Secret Key:**

```
flash001.py ×

flash001.py > ...
  1    from flask import Flask, render_template, redirect, url_for, flash
  2
  3    app = Flask(__name__)
  4    app.secret_key = 'your_secret_key'
```

**b. Define Routes:**

```
@app.route('/')
def index():
    return render_template('index.html')

@app.route('/flash-message')
def flash_message():
    flash("This is a flash message!", "info")
    return redirect(url_for('index'))
```

**c. HTML Template for Displaying Messages: Template File**

```
flash001.py        <> index.html  ×

templates > <> index.html > ...
   1    <!DOCTYPE html>
   2    <html lang="en">
   3    <head>
   4        <title>Flask Flash Messages</title>
   5        <style>
   6            .info { color: blue; }
   7            .success { color: green; }
   8            .error { color: red; }
   9        </style>
  10    </head>
  11    <body>
  12        <h1>Flask Flash Messages</h1>
  13        <a href="{{ url_for('flash_message') }}">Trigger Flash Message</a>
  14
  15        {% with messages = get_flashed_messages(with_categories=true) %}
  16            {% if messages %}
  17                <ul>
  18                    {% for category, message in messages %}
  19                        <li class="{{ category }}">{{ message }}</li>
  20                    {% endfor %}
  21                </ul>
  22            {% endif %}
  23        {% endwith %}
  24    </body>
  25    </html>
```

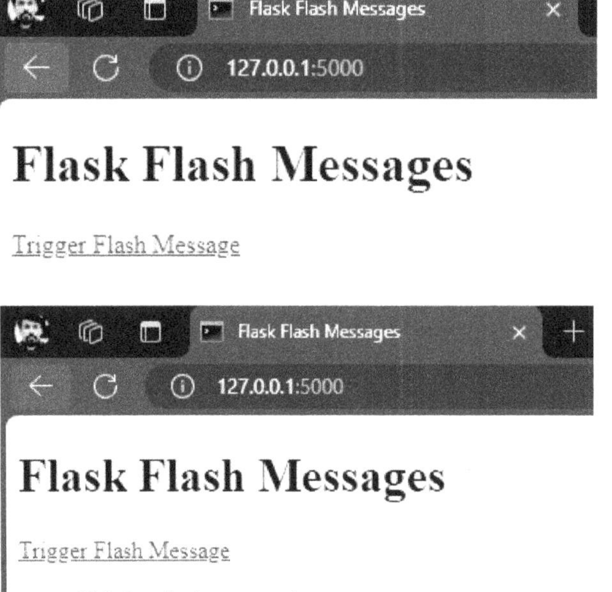


# Advanced Concepts

- **Multiple Messages**

Flask allows flashing multiple messages within the same request.

```python
@app.route('/multi-flash')
def multi_flash():
    flash("First message.", "success")
    flash("Second message.", "info")
    flash("Third message.", "error")
    return redirect(url_for('index'))
```

# Flask Flash Messages

Trigger Flash Message

- First message.
- **Second message.**
- Third message.

- **Using category_filter**

You can filter flashed messages by category when displaying them.

```
{% for category, message in get_flashed_messages(with_categories=true, category_filter=["error"]) %}
    <p class="error">{{ message }}</p>
{% endfor %}
```

- **Persistent Flash Messages**

If you need to persist flash messages for more than one request-response cycle, consider re-flashing them:

```python
messages = get_flashed_messages(with_categories=True)
for category, message in messages:
    flash(message, category)
```

- **Styling with CSS Frameworks**

Most CSS frameworks (e.g., Bootstrap, Tailwind) offer classes for alerts. Combine them with Flask's message categories for styled notifications.

Bootstrap Example: Template file

```
{% with messages = get_flashed_messages(with_categories=true) %}
{% if messages %}
<div class="alert-container">
    {% for category, message in messages %}
    <div class="alert alert-{{ category }}">
        {{ message }}
    </div>
    {% endfor %}
</div>
{% endif %}
{% endwith %}
```

Flask Flash with Bootstrap: application file

```
flash("This is a Bootstrap success alert!", "success")
flash("This is a Bootstrap error alert!", "danger")
```

Common Pitfalls

1. **Forgetting the Secret Key:**

   Without a secret_key, Flask will raise an error because sessions (and hence flashing) won't work.

2. **Not Redirecting After Flash:**

   If you flash a message without redirecting, it will be displayed on the current request and might be lost on page reload.

3. **Overloading the Session:**

   Flashing too many messages or large data can bloat the session cookie. Keep messages concise.

4. **Not Styling Categories:**

   If you don't style or handle categories in your template, all messages may look the same, leading to poor user experience.

# Full Example with a Form:

**Template File:**

```
flash003.py        <> index01.html  ×

templates > <> index01.html > ...
   1    <!DOCTYPE html>
   2    <html>
   3    <head>
   4        <title>Form Example</title>
   5    </head>
   6    <body>
   7        <form method="POST">
   8            <label for="username">Enter your name:</label>
   9            <input type="text" name="username" id="username">
  10            <button type="submit">Submit</button>
  11        </form>
  12
  13        {% with messages = get_flashed_messages(with_categories=true) %}
  14            {% if messages %}
  15                <ul>
  16                    {% for category, message in messages %}
  17                        <li class="{{ category }}">{{ message }}</li>
  18                    {% endfor %}
  19                </ul>
  20            {% endif %}
  21        {% endwith %}
  22    </body>
  23    </html>
```

## Application File:

```
flash003.py  ×    <> index01.html

flash003.py > index
   1    from flask import Flask, render_template, request, flash, redirect, url_for
   2
   3    app = Flask(__name__)
   4    app.secret_key = 'super_secret_key'
   5
   6    @app.route('/', methods=['GET', 'POST'])
   7    def index():
   8        if request.method == 'POST':
   9            username = request.form.get('username')
  10            if not username:
  11                flash("Username is required.", "error")
  12            else:
  13                flash(f"Welcome, {username}!", "success")
  14            return redirect(url_for('index'))
  15        return render_template('index01.html')
  16
  17    if __name__ == '__main__':
  18        app.run(debug=True)
```

## Another Example:

## Application file

```python
3   from flask import Flask, flash, redirect, render_template, request, url_for
4
5   app = Flask(__name__)
6   app.secret_key = 'a secrect key'
7
8   @app.route('/')
9   def index():
10      return render_template('index02.html')
11
12  @app.route('/login', methods = ['GET', 'POST'])
13  def login():
14      error = None
15      if request.method == 'POST':
16          if request.form['username'] != 'admin' or request.form['password'] != 'admin':
17              error = 'Invalid username or password. Please try again!'
18          else:
19              flash('You were successfully logged in')
20              return redirect(url_for('index'))
21      return render_template('login02.html', error = error)
22
23  if __name__ == "__main__":
24      app.run(debug = True)
25
```

## Template File:



```html
1   <!doctype html>
2   <html>
3
4   <head>
5       <title>Example for Flash Message</title>
6   </head>
7
8   <body>
9       {% with messages = get_flashed_messages() %}
10      {% if messages %}
11      <ul>
12          {% for message in messages %}
13          <li>{{ message }}</li>
14          {% endfor %}
15      </ul>
16      {% endif %}
17      {% endwith %}
18      <h1>Flask Message - Example</h1>
19      <p>To test please login. <br>Do you want to <a href="{{ url_for('login') }}"><b>log in?</b></a></p
20  </body>
21
22  </html>
```

```html
1    <!doctype html>
2    <html>
3       <body>
4          <h1>Login</h1>
5
6          {% if error %}
7             <p><strong>Error:</strong> {{ error }}
8          {% endif %}
9
10         <form action = "" method = "post">
11            <dl>
12               <dt>Username:</dt>
13               <dd>
14                  <input type = "text" name = "username"
15                     value = "{{request.form.username }}">
16               </dd>
17               <dt>Password:</dt>
18               <dd><input type = "password" name = "password"></dd>
19            </dl>
20            <p><input type = "submit" value = "Login"></p>
21         </form>
22      </body>
```

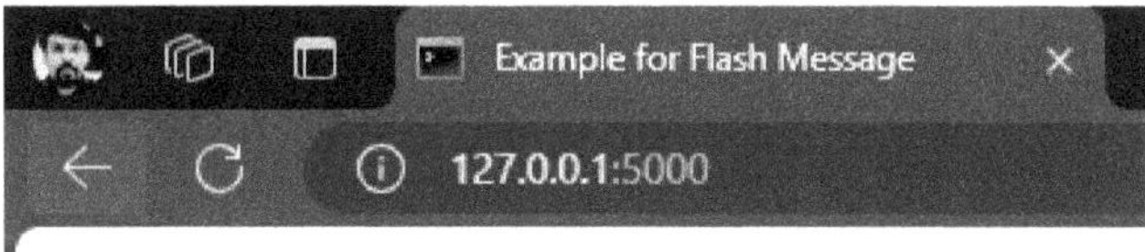


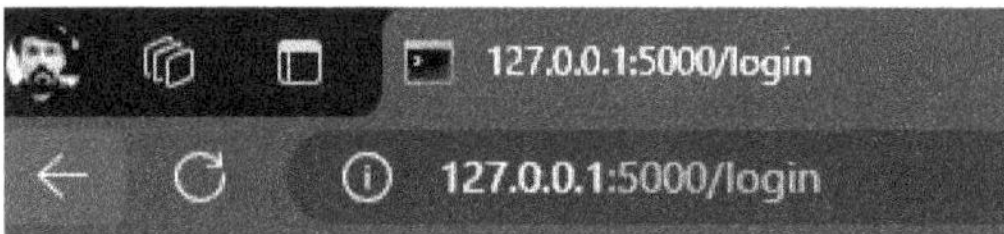


# Login

Username:
Somnath
Password:
•••••

Login

# Login

**Error:** Invalid username or password. Please try again!

Username:
Somnath

Password:

Login

On putting username and password as admin

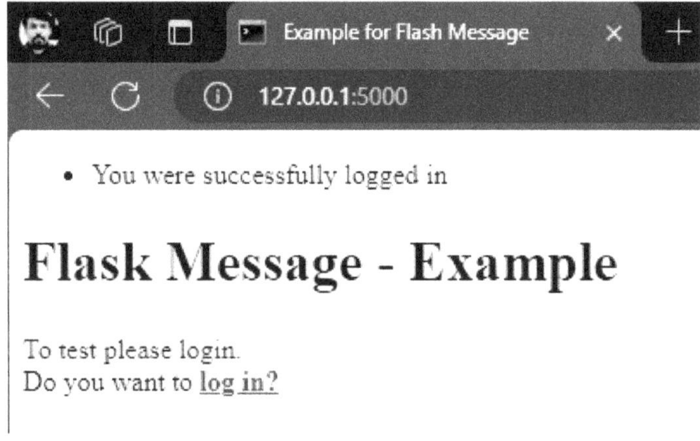

# 16. File Uploading

Uploading files in Flask is straightforward. It requires an HTML form with the enctype attribute set to multipart/form-data, which posts the file to a specified URL. The URL handler retrieves the file from the request.files[] object and saves it to the desired location.

Initially, each uploaded file is stored temporarily on the server before being moved to its destination. The destination file's name can either be hardcoded or derived from the filename property of the request.files[file] object. However, it is recommended to use the secure_filename() function to ensure a safe filename.

Additionally, you can configure the default upload folder path and the maximum allowed file size through the Flask object's configuration settings.

## Flask Setup for File Uploads:

Flask is a lightweight web framework that allows easy handling of HTTP requests, including file uploads. To enable file uploads in Flask, you must configure the app and handle the uploaded file data securely.

**Steps:**

1. **Install Flask**: Install Flask using pip if it is not already installed:

   a. pip install flask

2. **Directory Structure**: Create a directory for your Flask app. For example:

3. **File Handling**: Use Flask's request.files object to access files uploaded in HTTP POST requests.

Configuring the Flask App:

**Configuration Variables:**

1. **Upload Folder**: Specify where the uploaded files will be stored.

2. **Allowed Extensions**: Restrict file uploads to certain types (e.g., images, PDFs).

# Example Code:

```
uploads001.py  ×
uploads001.py > ...
   1    from flask import Flask
   2    import os
   3
   4    app = Flask(__name__)
   5
   6    # Set the directory where files will be uploaded
   7    UPLOAD_FOLDER = 'uploads'
   8    app.config['UPLOAD_FOLDER'] = UPLOAD_FOLDER
   9
  10    # Restrict to specific file extensions
  11    ALLOWED_EXTENSIONS = {'png', 'jpg', 'jpeg', 'gif', 'txt', 'pdf'}
  12
  13    # Ensure the folder exists
  14    if not os.path.exists(UPLOAD_FOLDER):
  15        os.makedirs(UPLOAD_FOLDER)
  16
```

## Function to Check Allowed File Types

To ensure only certain types of files can be uploaded, create a helper function that checks the file extension.

```
def allowed_file(filename):
    # Check if the file has a valid extension
    return '.' in filename and \
           filename.rsplit('.', 1)[1].lower() in ALLOWED_EXTENSIONS
```

**Explanation:**

1. **rsplit**: Splits the filename into two parts from the right at the first period (.).

2. **lower()**: Ensures case insensitivity (e.g., .JPG is treated the same as .jpg).

## Handling File Upload Requests

Use Flask's request object to process uploaded files. The request.files dictionary contains file objects submitted via forms.

## Example Route:

```
from flask import Flask, request, redirect, url_for, render_template, flash
```

```python
from werkzeug.utils import secure_filename
import os


app = Flask(__name__)
app.secret_key = 'your_secret_key'


# Set the directory where files will be uploaded
UPLOAD_FOLDER = 'uploads'
app.config['UPLOAD_FOLDER'] = UPLOAD_FOLDER


# Restrict to specific file extensions
ALLOWED_EXTENSIONS = {'png', 'jpg', 'jpeg', 'gif', 'txt', 'pdf'}


@app.route('/upload', methods=['GET', 'POST'])
def upload_file():
    if request.method == 'POST':
        # Check if the file part exists in the request
        if 'file' not in request.files:
            flash('No file part')
            return redirect(request.url)


        file = request.files['file']


        # Check if the user has selected a file
        if file.filename == '':
            flash('No file selected')
            return redirect(request.url)


        # Validate the file and save it
        if file and allowed_file(file.filename):
            filename = secure_filename(file.filename)  # Prevent malicious filenames
            file.save(os.path.join(app.config['UPLOAD_FOLDER'], filename))
            flash('File uploaded successfully!')
            return redirect(url_for('upload_file'))


    return render_template('upload.html')


def allowed_file(filename):
    # Check if the file has a valid extension
    return '.' in filename and \
```

```
filename.rsplit('.', 1)[1].lower() in ALLOWED_EXTENSIONS
```

# HTML Template for File Upload Form

Create an HTML form to allow users to upload files. The enctype="multipart/form-data" attribute is required for file uploads.

Code (templates/upload.html):

```
1   <!doctype html>
2   <html lang="en">
3   <head>
4       <title>File Upload</title>
5   </head>
6   <body>
7       <h1>Upload a File</h1>
8       {% with messages = get_flashed_messages() %}
9           {% if messages %}
10              <ul>
11                  {% for message in messages %}
12                      <li>{{ message }}</li>
13                  {% endfor %}
14              </ul>
15          {% endif %}
16      {% endwith %}
17      <form method="post" enctype="multipart/form-data">
18          <input type="file" name="file">
19          <input type="submit" value="Upload">
20      </form>
21  </body>
22  </html>
```

**Explanation:**

1. **enctype="multipart/form-data"**: Specifies that the form can send files.

2. **input type="file"**: Allows users to select files.

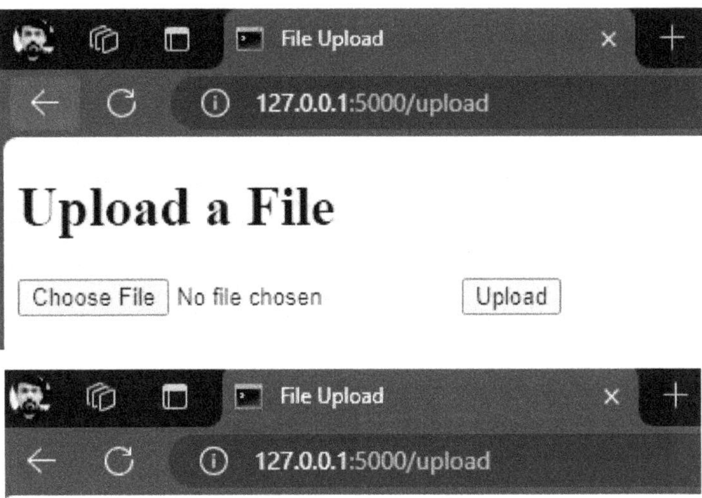

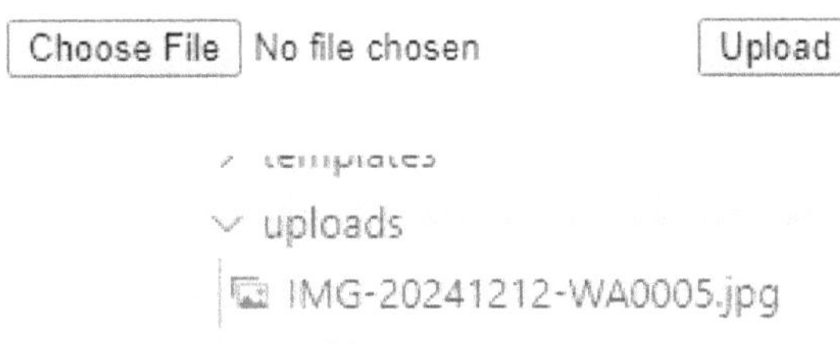

Uploaded in the folder uploads.

Securing File Uploads

**1. Sanitizing Filenames:**

Use secure_filename from werkzeug.utils to avoid directory traversal attacks.

```
29
30          # Validate the file and save it
31          if file and allowed_file(file.filename):
32              filename = secure_filename(file.filename)  # Prevent malicious filenames
```

Example:

- Unsafe Filename: ../../etc/passwd

- Sanitized Filename: etc_passwd

## Limiting File Sizes:

Prevent users from uploading excessively large files by setting MAX_CONTENT_LENGTH.

```python
app.config['MAX_CONTENT_LENGTH'] = 16 * 1024 * 1024  # 16MB
```

## Content Validation:

Optionally inspect file content to confirm it matches its extension.

# 17. The Extensions

## What are Flask Extensions?

Flask is commonly known as a microframework because its core functionality primarily includes **WSGI** and routing, powered by **Werkzeug**, and a template engine based on **Jinja2**. Additionally, Flask provides built-in support for cookies, sessions, and web helpers like **JSON** and static files. However, these features alone are not sufficient for building a comprehensive web application. This is where Flask extensions come into play.

Flask extensions enhance the framework's capabilities, allowing developers to add specific functionality to their applications. These extensions are Python modules designed to integrate seamlessly with Flask. The Flask Extension Registry serves as a directory listing the available extensions, which can be easily installed using the **pip** utility.

Flask extensions are Python libraries designed to extend Flask's core functionality. While Flask is a microframework with minimal built-in tools, extensions help developers add features without reinventing the wheel.

For example, if you need a database, Flask itself doesn't provide one, but extensions like Flask-SQLAlchemy or Flask-Peewee make database integration seamless.

- **Core Philosophy**: Flask's simplicity lies in being extensible rather than including everything by default.

- **Key Role**: Extensions handle tasks like database ORM, form validation, authentication, caching, email handling, and more.

## Why Use Flask Extensions?

- **Rapid Development:**

  - Extensions provide ready-to-use features, saving time in application development. For example:

  - Writing a REST API? Use **Flask-RESTful** instead of manually handling JSON responses and HTTP methods.

- **Modularity:**

  - Extensions let you include only the required functionality, keeping your app focused and lightweight.
    For example:

  - If you need caching, add **Flask-Caching**.

  - If you need real-time WebSocket communication, add **Flask-SocketIO**.

- **Community-Driven:**

  - Extensions are often created and maintained by experienced developers, ensuring:

- Best practices are followed.

- Frequent updates for bug fixes and new features.

- Solutions are tested and battle-hardened.

- **Ease of Integration:**

  o Extensions are designed to integrate directly into Flask's ecosystem. For example:

  - Add middleware functionality by simply initializing the extension and passing the Flask app object.

# Common Flask Extensions

- **Flask-SQLAlchemy**

  o **Purpose**: Adds support for the SQLAlchemy ORM.

  o **Features**:

  - Manage relational databases with ease.

  - Perform complex queries using Python objects.

  - Map database tables to Python classes.

pip install flask-sqlalchemy

```python
from flask import Flask
from flask_sqlalchemy import SQLAlchemy

app = Flask(__name__)
app.config['SQLALCHEMY_DATABASE_URI'] = 'sqlite:///example.db'
db = SQLAlchemy(app)

class User(db.Model):
    id = db.Column(db.Integer, primary_key=True)
    name = db.Column(db.String(80), nullable=False)
```

- **Flask-Migrate**

  o **Purpose**: Adds database migration capabilities.

  o **Features**:

  - Tracks changes in the database schema over time.

  - Enables upgrades and downgrades between schema versions.

PowerShell commands

flask db init  # Initialize migrations

flask db migrate -m "Added users table"

flask db upgrade  # Apply changes

- **Flask-WTF**

  o **Purpose**: Simplifies form handling with WTForms.

  o **Features**:

    - Built-in CSRF protection for secure forms.

    - Form validation with custom validators.

```
exten002.py ×

exten002.py > ...
  6    app = Flask(__name__)
  7    app.config['SECRET_KEY'] = 'your_secret_key'
  8
  9    class MyForm(FlaskForm):
 10        name = StringField('Name', validators=[DataRequired()])
 11        submit = SubmitField('Submit')
 12
 13    @app.route('/', methods=['GET', 'POST'])
 14    def index():
 15        form = MyForm()
 16        if form.validate_on_submit():
 17            return f'Hello, {form.name.data}!'
 18        return render_template('index.html', form=form)
 19
```

- **Flask-Bootstrap**

  o **Purpose**: Integrates Bootstrap for styling.

  o **Features**:

    - Makes it easy to use pre-built responsive layouts and components.

```
from flask_bootstrap import Bootstrap

app = Flask(__name__)
Bootstrap(app)
```

- **Flask-Login**

  o **Purpose**: Manages user authentication.

- o **Features**:
    - Session handling.
    - Login/logout flow.
    - Protect routes with decorators like @login_required.

```
                    pip install flask-login

        from flask_login import LoginManager, UserMixin

        login_manager = LoginManager()
        login_manager.init_app(app)

        class User(UserMixin):
            pass
```

- **Flask-Mail**

  - **Purpose**: Facilitates email sending.

  - **Features**:
    - Configurable SMTP server settings.
    - Sending plain text and HTML emails.

```
from flask_mail import Mail, Message

mail = Mail(app)
msg = Message('Hello', sender='you@example.com', recipients=['recipient@example.com'])
msg.body = "This is the email body"
mail.send(msg)
```

- **Flask-Caching**

  - o **Purpose**: Improves app performance by caching responses.

  - o **Features**:
    - Supports multiple backends like Redis, Memcached, and local memory.

```
        from flask_caching import Cache

        cache = Cache(app, config={'CACHE_TYPE': 'simple'})
```

- **Flask-RESTful**

  - o **Purpose**: Simplifies the creation of REST APIs.

  - o **Features**:

- Manage endpoints using classes.
- Handle JSON serialization automatically.

```
pip install flask-restful

from flask_restful import Api, Resource

api = Api(app)

class HelloWorld(Resource):
    def get(self):
        return {'message': 'Hello, World!'}

api.add_resource(HelloWorld, '/')
```

- **Flask-SocketIO**
  - **Purpose**: Adds WebSocket support for real-time communication.
  - **Features**:
    - Enables push notifications, chat apps, and more.

```
from flask_socketio import SocketIO

socketio = SocketIO(app)
```

- **Flask-CORS**
  - Purpose: Solves cross-origin request issues.
  - Features:
    - Customize allowed origins, headers, and methods.

```
pip install flask_cors

from flask_cors import CORS
CORS(app)
```

# How to Install Flask Extensions

Extensions are usually installed via pip. Use the following format:

```
pip install <extension-name>
```

For example:

```
pip install flask-sqlalchemy
pip install flask-wtf
```

# How to Find Flask Extensions

**Official Extensions:**

- Visit the Flask Extensions Registry.

**Third-Party Extensions:**

- Search on PyPI or GitHub. Look for Flask-specific libraries.

Best Practices for Using Flask Extensions

- Use Only What You Need

    o Avoid bloating your app by installing unnecessary extensions. For instance:

        ▪ Only use Flask-Caching if caching improves performance.

- Check Compatibility

    o Ensure your Flask version is compatible with the extension.

- Keep Updated

    o Extensions are frequently updated. Use:

        ▪ pip install --upgrade <extension-name>

- Documentation

    o Always refer to the official documentation. Each extension has its unique configuration and API.

- Build Custom Extensions

    o If an existing extension doesn't meet your requirements, you can build a custom extension.

Some of the Extensions are discussed in detail in the next chapters.

# 18. The Flask-Mail

**Flask-Mail** is an extension for Flask applications that simplifies the process of sending emails. It integrates seamlessly with Flask, allowing developers to configure email settings, compose emails, and send them programmatically. **Flask-Mail** extension makes it very easy to set up a simple interface with any email server.

## Installation

a. To get started, you need to install Flask-Mail using pip:

  i. pip install Flask-Mail

b. This command downloads and installs the extension along with its dependencies.

## Configuration

a. Before using Flask-Mail, you need to configure your Flask app with the required email settings.

b. Basic Configuration

  i. Here is an example of configuring Flask-Mail for a Gmail SMTP server:

```python
from flask import Flask
from flask_mail import Mail

app = Flask(__name__)

# Flask-Mail Configuration
app.config['MAIL_SERVER'] = 'smtp.gmail.com'
app.config['MAIL_PORT'] = 587
app.config['MAIL_USE_TLS'] = True
app.config['MAIL_USE_SSL'] = False
app.config['MAIL_USERNAME'] = 'your_email@gmail.com'
app.config['MAIL_PASSWORD'] = 'your_password'
app.config['MAIL_DEFAULT_SENDER'] = 'your_email@gmail.com'

mail = Mail(app)
```

- **MAIL_SERVER**: The address of the email server (e.g., smtp.gmail.com for Gmail).

- **MAIL_PORT**: Port for communication. Use 587 for TLS or 465 for SSL.

- **MAIL_USE_TLS**: Enables Transport Layer Security.

- **MAIL_USE_SSL**: Enables Secure Sockets Layer.

- **MAIL_USERNAME**: Your email address (sender email).

- **MAIL_PASSWORD**: Password or app-specific password for your email account.

- **MAIL_DEFAULT_SENDER**: Default "From" address for emails.

# Example Using Environment Variables

Storing sensitive information like email credentials in code is not recommended. Use environment variables instead:

```python
import os


app.config['MAIL_USERNAME'] = os.getenv('MAIL_USERNAME')
app.config['MAIL_PASSWORD'] = os.getenv('MAIL_PASSWORD')
```

Sending Emails

    a.  **Sending a Simple Email**

        ii.  Use the Message class to create an email and the send() method to dispatch it.

```python
app = Flask(__name__)
mail = Mail(app)


@app.route('/send_email')
def send_email():
    msg = Message(
        subject="Hello from Flask-Mail!",
        recipients=['recipient@example.com'],  # List of recipient emails
        body="This is a plain text email sent from Flask-Mail."
    )
    mail.send(msg)
    return "Email sent successfully!"
```

       iii.  Explanation:

          1.  subject: Email subject line.

          2.  recipients: A list of recipients.

          3.  body: Plain text content for the email.

# Sending HTML Emails

    a.  Flask-Mail supports HTML content for richer emails. Use the html parameter:

```python
from flask import Flask, url_for
from flask_mail import Mail, Message


app = Flask(__name__)
```

```python
# Flask-Mail Configuration
app.config['MAIL_SERVER'] = 'smtp.gmail.com'
app.config['MAIL_PORT'] = 587
app.config['MAIL_USE_TLS'] = True
app.config['MAIL_USE_SSL'] = False
app.config['MAIL_USERNAME'] = 'your_email@gmail.com'
app.config['MAIL_PASSWORD'] = 'your_password'
app.config['MAIL_DEFAULT_SENDER'] = 'your_email@gmail.com'

mail = Mail(app)

@app.route('/send_html_email')
def send_html_email():
    msg = Message(
        subject="HTML Email Example",
        recipients=['recipient@example.com'],
        html="<h1>Welcome!</h1><p>This is an <strong>HTML email</strong>.</p>"
    )
    mail.send(msg)
    return "HTML Email sent!"
```

b.  Use Case:

  iv.  HTML emails are great for sending newsletters, branded communication, or formatted content.

Sending Emails with Attachments

a.  You can attach files to emails using the attach() method.

```python
@app.route('/send_email_with_attachment')
def send_email_with_attachment():
    msg = Message(
        subject="Email with Attachment",
        recipients=['recipient@example.com'],
        body="Please find the attached file."
    )
    with app.open_resource('example.pdf') as pdf:
        msg.attach("example.pdf", "application/pdf", pdf.read())
    mail.send(msg)
    return "Email with attachment sent!"
```

b.  Explanation:

  v.  open_resource(): Opens the file to attach.

vi.   attach(): Adds the file to the email

## Error Handling

a.   To prevent crashes, wrap email-sending logic in a try-except block:

```python
@app.route('/send_email_safe')
def send_email_safe():
    msg = Message(
        subject="Safe Email",
        recipients=['recipient@example.com'],
        body="This email demonstrates error handling."
    )
    try:
        mail.send(msg)
        return "Email sent successfully!"
    except Exception as e:
        return f"Failed to send email: {str(e)}"
```

## Testing Emails

a.   Flask-Mail allows testing email functionality using a console backend. This avoids sending real emails during development.

```python
app.config['MAIL_SUPPRESS_SEND'] = False  # Suppresses sending emails
app.config['MAIL_DEBUG'] = True   # Enables debug messages
app.config['MAIL_BACKEND'] = 'console'   # Prints emails to the console
```

b.   Example Output in Console:

```
Subject: Safe Email
To: recipient@example.com
Body:
This email demonstrates error handling.
```

# Common Use Cases

a.   User Registration Confirmation

vii.   Send an email when a user registers successfully:

```python
@app.route('/register_user')
def register_user():
    # Simulate user registration
    user_email = 'user@example.com'
    msg = Message(
        subject="Welcome to Our Platform!",
        recipients=[user_email],
        body="Thank you for registering. Enjoy our services!"
    )
    mail.send(msg)
    return "Registration confirmation email sent!"
```

b. Password Reset

viii. Send password reset instructions:

```python
@app.route('/reset_password')
def reset_password():
    user_email = 'user@example.com'
    reset_link = "https://example.com/reset?token=abc123"
    msg = Message(
        subject="Password Reset Request",
        recipients=[user_email],
        html=f"<p>Click the link below to reset your password:</p>
        <a href='{reset_link}'>Reset Password</a>"
    )
    mail.send(msg)
    return "Password reset email sent!"
```

# Security Best Practices

a. Avoid Hardcoding Credentials Use environment variables or configuration management tools to store sensitive data.

b. Use Application-Specific Passwords for Gmail, generate an app-specific password instead of using your account password.

c. Enable SSL/TLS Always to use secure protocols (TLS/SSL) to prevent data interception.

d. Monitor Email Sending Keep track of errors and bounce rates to ensure smooth delivery.

Flask-Mail is an essential tool for sending emails from Flask applications. By leveraging its rich feature set, you can enhance your web application's communication capabilities—be it for user notifications, promotional emails, or administrative alerts. Proper configuration and security measures ensure smooth and secure email delivery.

# 19. WTF Forms

WTF Forms (Flask-WTF) is a Python extension for Flask that integrates seamlessly with **WTForms**, a library for handling web forms. It simplifies form validation, CSRF protection, and rendering in Flask applications. A key component of a web application is presenting a user interface to interact with users. HTML provides the <form> tag, which is used to design such interfaces. Form elements like text inputs, radio buttons, and dropdown menus (select) can be utilized as needed.

When a user submits data, it is sent to the server as an HTTP request, using either the GET or POST method. However, this process has some drawbacks:

- The server-side script must reconstruct the form elements from the HTTP request data, meaning the form elements need to be defined twice—once in HTML and again in the server-side script.

- HTML forms have limited flexibility for dynamic rendering of form elements and lack built-in mechanisms for input validation.

This is where **WTForms** becomes useful. **WTForms** is a versatile library for form rendering and validation. The Flask-WTF extension simplifies integration with **WTForms** in Flask applications.

With Flask-WTF, you can define form fields directly in your Python script and render them in an HTML template. Additionally, it allows you to apply validation rules to form fields efficiently.

## Installation

Flask-WTF is an extension that combines Flask's capabilities with WTForms.

To use it, install it using pip:

**Installation**

- Flask-WTF is an extension that combines Flask's capabilities with WTForms.
  - To use it, install it using pip:

```
pip install flask-wtf
```

  - It also installs WTForms as a dependency.

- Key Dependencies:
  - **Flask**: The web framework.
  - **WTForms**: A library for form handling.

Key Features

- Flask-WTF offers the following key features:
  - Form Management:
    - Helps create Python classes for forms instead of manually handling form data.

- Automatically handles validation and form binding.
  - o CSRF Protection:
    - Automatically injects a hidden token into forms for CSRF protection.
    - Protects against malicious form submissions from other sites.
  - o Field Validation:
    - Includes a wide variety of built-in validators like DataRequired, Email, and Length.
    - Supports custom validation logic for flexibility.
  - o Dynamic Form Rendering:
    - Works seamlessly with Flask's Jinja2 templating engine for easy form rendering.
  - o Custom Widgets:
    - Enables customization of how fields are displayed in the front end.

# Basic Usage

- Setup
  - o Import Flask, Flask-WTF, and WTForms modules.
  - o Set up the Flask app with a secret key for CSRF protection.
  - o Example:

```
wtf001.py
wtf001.py > ...
1    from flask import Flask
2    from flask_wtf import FlaskForm
3    from wtforms import StringField, PasswordField, SubmitField
4
5    app = Flask(__name__)
6    app.config['SECRET_KEY'] = 'your_secret_key'
```

  - o This setup ensures your app is ready to create and process forms.

# Defining a Form

- Forms in Flask-WTF are defined by creating Python classes that inherit from FlaskForm.
- Example:

```python
from flask import Flask, render_template, request
from flask_wtf import FlaskForm
from wtforms import StringField, PasswordField, SubmitField
from wtforms.validators import DataRequired, Email


app = Flask(__name__)
app.config['SECRET_KEY'] = 'your_secret_key'


class LoginForm(FlaskForm):
    email = StringField('Email', validators=[DataRequired(), Email()])
    password = PasswordField('Password', validators=[DataRequired()])
    submit = SubmitField('Login')
```

- Explanation:

  - Fields:

    - StringField: A single-line text input.

    - PasswordField: A single-line password input.

    - SubmitField: A button to submit the form.

  - Validators:

    - DataRequired: Ensures the field is not empty.

    - Email: Validates the format of the email input.

# Handling a Form

- The form is processed in a Flask route. You validate the form and handle the submitted data.

- Example:

```python
@app.route('/login', methods=['GET', 'POST'])
def login():
    form = LoginForm()
    if form.validate_on_submit():
        email = form.email.data
        password = form.password.data
        return f"Logged in as {email}"
    return render_template('login.html', form=form)
```

- Key Functions:

  - form.validate_on_submit(): Checks if the form was submitted and passes validation.

Rendering in Jinja2

- Forms are rendered in templates using Jinja2.

- Example:

```
templates > <> wtf001.html > ...
1   <form method="post">
2       {{ form.hidden_tag() }}
3       <p>{{ form.email.label }} {{ form.email() }}</p>
4       <p>{{ form.password.label }} {{ form.password() }}</p>
5       <p>{{ form.submit() }}</p>
6   </form>
```

- form.hidden_tag(): Adds the CSRF token.

- form.field_name(): Renders the HTML input field.

Common Field Types

- WTForms provides various field types to cater to different input requirements:

  o **Text Fields:**

    - **StringField:** Single-line input.

    - **PasswordField:** Input for passwords (hidden text).

  o **Text Area:**

    - **TextAreaField:** Multi-line input.

  o **Selection:**

    - **SelectField:** Dropdown menu.

    - **RadioField:** Radio buttons.

  o **Boolean:**

    - **BooleanField:** Checkbox input.

  o **File Uploads:**

    - **FileField:** Handles file uploads.

  o **Submit:**

    - **SubmitField:** Adds a submit button.

- Example:

```python
 1  from flask import Flask, render_template, request
 2  from flask_wtf import FlaskForm
 3  from wtforms import StringField, PasswordField, SubmitField, TextAreaField, BooleanField
 4  from wtforms.validators import DataRequired, Email
 5
 6
 7  app = Flask(__name__)
 8  app.config['SECRET_KEY'] = 'your_secret_key'
 9
10  class LoginForm(FlaskForm):
11      email = StringField('Email', validators=[DataRequired(), Email()])
12      password = PasswordField('Password', validators=[DataRequired()])
13      submit = SubmitField('Login')
14
15  class ExampleForm(FlaskForm):
16      comments = TextAreaField('Comments')
17      agree = BooleanField('I Agree')
18      submit = SubmitField('Submit')
```

# Built-in Validators

- Validators ensure that form input meets specific requirements. Common validators include:

    o **DataRequired**: Ensures input is not empty.

    o **Email**: Validates email format.

    o **Length**: Restricts the length of input.

    o **Regexp**: Matches input to a regex pattern.

    o **NumberRange**: Ensures numbers fall within a range.

- Example:

```python
 1  from flask import Flask, render_template, request
 2  from flask_wtf import FlaskForm
 3  from wtforms import StringField, PasswordField, SubmitField, TextAreaField, BooleanField
 4  from wtforms.validators import DataRequired, Email, Length
 5
 6
 7  app = Flask(__name__)
 8  app.config['SECRET_KEY'] = 'your_secret_key'
 9
10  class LoginForm(FlaskForm):
11      email = StringField('Email', validators=[DataRequired(), Email()])
12      password = PasswordField('Password', validators=[DataRequired()])
13      submit = SubmitField('Login')
14
15  class ExampleForm(FlaskForm):
16      comments = TextAreaField('Comments')
17      agree = BooleanField('I Agree')
18      submit = SubmitField('Submit')
19
20
21  class UsernameForm(FlaskForm):
22      username = StringField('Username', validators=[DataRequired(), Length(min=4, max=25)])
23
```

## Custom Validation

- Create your own validation logic by defining custom validators.
- Example:

```python
from wtforms import ValidationError

def check_username(form, field):
    if field.data != "admin":
        raise ValidationError("Invalid username!")

class CustomForm(FlaskForm):
    username = StringField('Username', validators=[check_username])
```

## Complete Code:

```python
from flask import Flask, render_template, request
from flask_wtf import FlaskForm
from wtforms import StringField, PasswordField, SubmitField, TextAreaField, BooleanField
from wtforms.validators import DataRequired, Email, Length
from wtforms import ValidationError


app = Flask(__name__)
app.config['SECRET_KEY'] = 'your_secret_key'


class LoginForm(FlaskForm):
    email = StringField('Email', validators=[DataRequired(), Email()])
    password = PasswordField('Password', validators=[DataRequired()])
    submit = SubmitField('Login')


class ExampleForm(FlaskForm):
    comments = TextAreaField('Comments')
    agree = BooleanField('I Agree')
    submit = SubmitField('Submit')



class UsernameForm(FlaskForm):
    username = StringField('Username', validators=[DataRequired(), Length(min=4, max=25)])


def check_username(form, field):
    if field.data != "admin":
        raise ValidationError("Invalid username!")
```

```python
class CustomForm(FlaskForm):
    username = StringField('Username', validators=[check_username])


@app.route('/login', methods=['GET', 'POST'])
def login():
    form = LoginForm()
    if form.validate_on_submit():
        email = form.email.data
        password = form.password.data
        return f"Logged in as {email}"
    return render_template('login.html', form=form)
```

## CSRF Protection

- Flask-WTF automatically protects forms against CSRF attacks. Include {{ form.hidden_tag() }} in templates for the CSRF token.

- **Disable CSRF Protection**: To disable CSRF protection for a specific form:

```python
class NoCSRFForm(FlaskForm):
    class Meta:
        csrf = False
```

## File Uploads

- Handle file uploads by using FileField and werkzeug.utils.secure_filename.

- **Example:**

```
wtf002.py  ✕

wtf002.py > ...
 1   from flask import Flask, render_template, request
 2   from flask_wtf import FlaskForm
 3   from wtforms import FileField, SubmitField
 4   from werkzeug.utils import secure_filename
 5
 6   app = Flask(__name__)
 7   app.config['SECRET_KEY'] = 'your_secret_key'
 8
 9   class UploadForm(FlaskForm):
10       file = FileField('Upload File')
11       submit = SubmitField('Upload')
12
13   @app.route('/upload', methods=['GET', 'POST'])
14   def upload():
15       form = UploadForm()
16       if form.validate_on_submit():
17           f = form.file.data
18           filename = secure_filename(f.filename)
19           f.save(f"/path/to/uploads/{filename}")
20           return "File uploaded!"
21       return render_template('upload.html', form=form)
22
23   if __name__ == "__main__":
24     app.run(debug = True)
```

# Error Handling

- Flask-WTF provides detailed error messages when validation fails.

- Example:

```
{% for error in form.username.errors %}
    <div class="error">{{ error }}</div>
{% endfor %}
```

# Advanced Customization

- Customize forms and fields dynamically or with custom widgets.

- Dynamic Fields Example:

```python
class DynamicForm(FlaskForm):
    def __init__(self, fields):
        super().__init__()
        for name, field in fields.items():
            setattr(self, name, field)
```

- Custom Widget Example:

```python
from wtforms.widgets import TextInput

class CustomWidget(TextInput):
    def __call__(self, field, **kwargs):
        kwargs['class'] = 'custom-input'
        return super().__call__(field, **kwargs)
```

# Common Errors

- CSRF Token Missing:

    o   Ensure {{ form.hidden_tag() }} is included in your form template.

- Field Name Mismatch:

    o   Ensure field names in the template match those in the form class.

- Form Not Submitting:

    o   Verify the method is set to POST in the form tag: <form method="post">.

# More Example:

**Application File:**

```python
from flask import Flask, render_template, request
from flask_wtf import FlaskForm
from wtforms import StringField, PasswordField, BooleanField, IntegerField
from wtforms import DecimalField, RadioField, SelectField, TextAreaField, FileField
from wtforms.validators import InputRequired
from werkzeug.security import generate_password_hash


app = Flask(__name__)
app.config['SECRET_KEY'] = 'my secret key'


class MyForm(FlaskForm):
```

```python
    name = StringField('Name', validators=[InputRequired()])
    age = IntegerField('Age', validators=[InputRequired()])
    password = PasswordField('Password', validators=[InputRequired()])
    remember_me = BooleanField('Remember me')
    income = DecimalField('Annual Income', validators=[InputRequired()])
    gender = RadioField('Gender', choices=[
                    ('male', 'Male'), ('female', 'Female')])
    department = SelectField('Department', choices=[('GEN', 'General'), ('MIN', 'Medicine
Internal'),
                                        ('LIV', 'Liver')])
    message = TextAreaField('Message', validators=[InputRequired()])
    document = FileField('Document')


@app.route('/', methods=['GET', 'POST'])
def index():
    form = MyForm()
    if form.validate_on_submit():
        name = form.name.data
        age = form.age.data
        password = form.password.data
        remember_me = form.remember_me.data
        income = form.income.data
        gender = form.gender.data
        department = form.department.data
        message = form.message.data
        document = form.document.data.filename

        return f'''
        <table border=1>
            <tr>
                <td>Field</td>
                <td>Value</td>
            </tr>
            <tr>
                <td>Name</td>
                <td>{name}</td>
            </tr>
            <tr>
                <td>Age</td>
                <td>{age}</td>
            </tr>
```

```python
        <tr>
            <td>Password</td>
            <td>{generate_password_hash(password)}</td>
        </tr>
        <tr>
            <td>Remember me</td>
            <td>{remember_me}</td>
        </tr>
        <tr>
            <td>Annual Income</td>
            <td>{income}</td>
        </tr>
        <tr>
            <td>Gender</td>
            <td>{gender}</td>
        </tr>
        <tr>
            <td>Department</td>
            <td>{department}</td>
        </tr>
        <tr>
            <td>Message</td>
            <td>{message}</td>
        </tr>
        <tr>
            <td>Document</td>
            <td>{document}</td>
        </tr>
    </table>
    '''

    return render_template('index.html', form=form)


if __name__ == '__main__':
    app.run()
```

## Template File: index.html:

```html
<!DOCTYPE html>
<html>
<head>
    <title>Patient Registration Form</title>
```

```html
</head>
<body>
    <h1>Patient Registration Form</h1>
    <form method="post" action="/" enctype="multipart/form-data">
        {{ form.csrf_token }}
        <table>
            <tr>
                <td>{{ form.name.label }}</td>
                <td>:</td>
                <td>{{ form.name() }}</td>
            </tr>
            <tr>
                <td>{{ form.age.label }}</td>
                <td>:</td>
                <td>{{ form.age() }}</td>
            </tr>
            <tr>
                <td>{{ form.password.label }}</td>
                <td>:</td>
                <td>{{ form.password() }}</td>
            </tr>
            <tr>
                <td>{{ form.remember_me.label }}</td>
                <td>:</td>
                <td>{{ form.remember_me() }}</td>
            </tr>
            <tr>
                <td>{{ form.income.label }}</td>
                <td>:</td>
                <td>{{ form.income() }}</td>
            </tr>
            <tr>
                <td>{{ form.gender.label }}</td>
                <td>:</td>
                <td>{{ form.gender() }}</td>
            </tr>
            <tr>
                <td>{{ form.department.label }}</td>
                <td>:</td>
                <td>{{ form.department() }}</td>
            </tr>
```

```
        <tr>
            <td>{{ form.message.label }}</td>
            <td>:</td>
            <td>{{ form.message() }}</td>
        </tr>
        <tr>
            <td>{{ form.document.label }}</td>
            <td>:</td>
            <td>{{ form.document() }}</td>
        </tr>
        <tr>
            <td colspan="3"><input type="submit" value="Submit"></td>
        </tr>
    </table>
  </form>
</body>
</html>
```

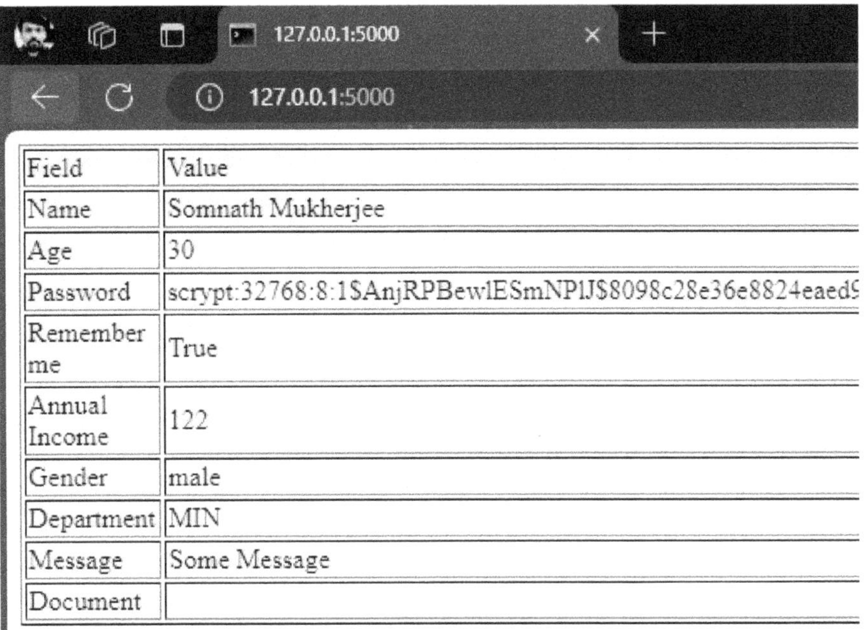

| Field | Value |
| --- | --- |
| Name | Somnath Mukherjee |
| Age | 30 |
| Password | scrypt:32768:8:1$AnjRPBewlESmNPlJ$8098c28e36e8824eaed9 |
| Remember me | True |
| Annual Income | 122 |
| Gender | male |
| Department | MIN |
| Message | Some Message |
| Document | |

# 20. SQLite

**SQLite** is a lightweight, serverless database that is an excellent choice for small to medium-sized applications. When combined with Flask, a micro web framework in Python, it offers an easy and efficient way to manage data in web applications. Python includes built-in support for SQLite, with the 'sqlite3' module being part of the standard Python distribution.

## Why SQLite with Flask?

- SQLite is ideal for Flask applications because:
  - **Ease of Use**: No need for complex setup; a single database file (database.db) is sufficient.
  - **Quick Prototyping**: Perfect for proof-of-concept applications.
  - **Lightweight**: Runs with minimal resource requirements.
  - **Portability**: The entire database is stored in a file, making it easy to share or deploy.
  - **Example**: Imagine you are developing a simple blog application. Instead of configuring a full database server like PostgreSQL, SQLite allows you to manage posts and users directly using a file-based database.
  - $ ls
  - app.py  database.db  schema.sql

## Setting Up SQLite in Flask

- **Basic App Configuration**:
  - Create a Flask app with SQLite connectivity:

```python
from flask import Flask, g
import sqlite3

app = Flask(__name__)
DATABASE = 'blog.db'

def get_db():
    """Connect to SQLite database."""
    db = getattr(g, '_database', None)
    if db is None:
        db = g._database = sqlite3.connect(DATABASE)
        db.row_factory = sqlite3.Row  # To access rows as dictionaries
    return db
```

```python
@app.teardown_appcontext
def close_connection(exception):
    """Close the database connection."""
    db = getattr(g, '_database', None)
    if db is not None:
        db.close()


@app.route('/')
def index():
    return "Welcome to the Blog!"


if __name__ == '__main__':
    app.run()
```

## Database Schema and Initialization

- Schema Design

    o For a blogging app, the schema could look like this:

```sql
-- schema.sql
CREATE TABLE users (
    id INTEGER PRIMARY KEY AUTOINCREMENT,
    username TEXT NOT NULL UNIQUE,
    email TEXT NOT NULL UNIQUE,
    password TEXT NOT NULL
);

CREATE TABLE posts (
    id INTEGER PRIMARY KEY AUTOINCREMENT,
    user_id INTEGER NOT NULL,
    title TEXT NOT NULL,
    content TEXT NOT NULL,
    created_at TIMESTAMP DEFAULT CURRENT_TIMESTAMP,
    FOREIGN KEY (user_id) REFERENCES users (id)
);
```

- Initializing the Database

    o Write a script to initialize the database:

```python
def get_db():
    """Connect to SQLite database."""
    db = getattr(g, '_database', None)
    if db is None:
        db = g._database = sqlite3.connect(DATABASE)
        db.row_factory = sqlite3.Row  # To access rows as dictionaries
    return db

if __name__ == '__main__':
    init_db()
```

Run the command in the command window:

$ python init_db.py

Database initialized!

This will create a database named as blog.db

```
  blog.db
  schema.sql
  sqlite001.py
```

Performing CRUD Operations

- **Create**

    - Add a new user:

        ```python
        from flask import request, jsonify

        @app.route('/add_user', methods=['POST'])
        def add_user():
            data = request.json
            query = "INSERT INTO users (username, email, password) VALUES (?, ?, ?)"
            values = (data['username'], data['email'], data['password'])
            db = get_db()
            cursor = db.cursor()
            try:
                cursor.execute(query, values)
                db.commit()
                return jsonify({"message": "User added successfully!"}), 201
            except sqlite3.IntegrityError:
                return jsonify({"error": "Username or email already exists!"}), 400
        ```

    - Data could be collected by using POST method called from a Template.

- **Read**

    - Retrieve all users:

```python
@app.route('/users', methods=['GET'])
def get_users():
    query = "SELECT id, username, email FROM users"
    db = get_db()
    cursor = db.cursor()
    cursor.execute(query)
    users = cursor.fetchall()
    return jsonify([dict(user) for user in users])
```

**Example Response:**

```
[
    {"id": 1, "username": "john_doe", "email": "john@example.com"},
    {"id": 2, "username": "jane_doe", "email": "jane@example.com"}
]
```

- **Update**

  o Update user details:

```python
@app.route('/update_user/<int:user_id>', methods=['PUT'])
def update_user(user_id):
    data = request.json
    query = "UPDATE users SET username = ?, email = ?, password = ? WHERE id = ?"
    values = (data['username'], data['email'], data['password'], user_id)
    db = get_db()
    cursor = db.cursor()
    cursor.execute(query, values)
    db.commit()
    return jsonify({"message": "User updated successfully!"})
```

- **Delete**

  o Delete a user:

```python
@app.route('/delete_user/<int:user_id>', methods=['DELETE'])
def delete_user(user_id):
    query = "DELETE FROM users WHERE id = ?"
    db = get_db()
    cursor = db.cursor()
    cursor.execute(query, (user_id,))
    db.commit()
    return jsonify({"message": "User deleted successfully!"})
```

# Best Practices

- **Avoid SQL Injection**: Use parameterized queries or ORM to prevent SQL injection vulnerabilities.

- **Connection Management**: Use Flask's g object to manage database connections efficiently and close them when the request ends.

- **Migration Tools**: Use Flask-Migrate to handle schema updates:

```
pip install flask-migrate
flask db init
flask db migrate -m "Add new table"
flask db upgrade
```

- **Environment Separation**: Use separate databases for development (dev.db), testing (test.db), and production (prod.db).

# Example Application:

Now we learned enough so as we can create an application.

Here is a complete Flask application with templates using SQLite for CRUD operations in the context of a Blog Application. This example includes HTML templates for rendering pages and handling user interactions.

- **Directory Structure**

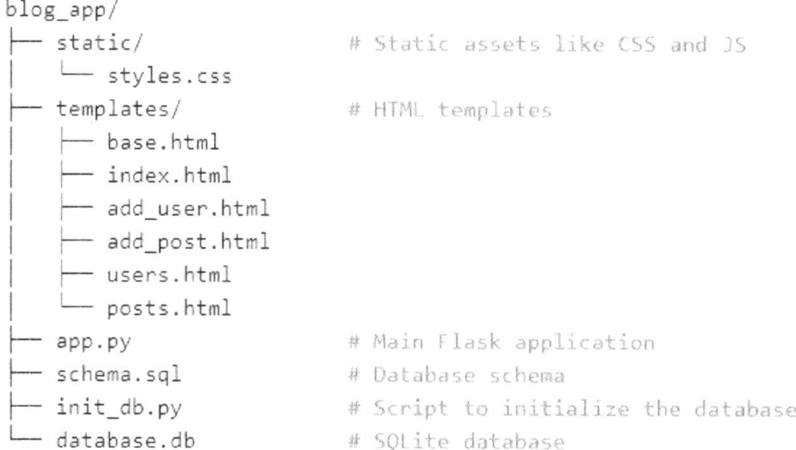

```
blog_app/
├── static/                 # Static assets like CSS and JS
│   └── styles.css
├── templates/              # HTML templates
│   ├── base.html
│   ├── index.html
│   ├── add_user.html
│   ├── add_post.html
│   ├── users.html
│   └── posts.html
├── app.py                  # Main Flask application
├── schema.sql              # Database schema
├── init_db.py              # Script to initialize the database
└── database.db             # SQLite database
```

- **Schema Definition**

    o   Create a file schema.sql to define the database schema:

```
schema.sql  ×
schema.sql
  2    CREATE TABLE users (
  3        id INTEGER PRIMARY KEY AUTOINCREMENT,
  4        username TEXT NOT NULL UNIQUE,
  5        email TEXT NOT NULL UNIQUE,
  6        password TEXT NOT NULL
  7    );
  8
  9    CREATE TABLE posts (
 10        id INTEGER PRIMARY KEY AUTOINCREMENT,
 11        user_id INTEGER NOT NULL,
 12        title TEXT NOT NULL,
 13        content TEXT NOT NULL,
 14        created_at TIMESTAMP DEFAULT CURRENT_TIMESTAMP,
 15        FOREIGN KEY (user_id) REFERENCES users (id)
 16    ):
```

- **Database Initialization**

    o  Create a file init_db.py to initialize the database:

```
schema.sql        init_db.py  ×
init_db.py > ...
  1    import sqlite3
  2
  3    def init_db():
  4        """Initialize the SQLite database."""
  5        with sqlite3.connect('database.db') as conn:
  6            with open('schema.sql', 'r') as f:
  7                conn.executescript(f.read())
  8        print("Database initialized!")
  9
 10    if __name__ == '__main__':
 11        init_db()
```

- Run the script:

```
python init_db.py
```

- **Flask Application**:

    o  Create the main application file app.py:

```
from flask import Flask, render_template, request, redirect, url_for, g
import sqlite3


app = Flask(__name__)
DATABASE = 'database.db'
```

```python
def get_db():
    """Connect to SQLite database."""
    db = getattr(g, '_database', None)
    if db is None:
        db = g._database = sqlite3.connect(DATABASE)
        db.row_factory = sqlite3.Row
    return db


@app.teardown_appcontext
def close_connection(exception):
    """Close the database connection."""
    db = getattr(g, '_database', None)
    if db is not None:
        db.close()


@app.route('/')
def index():
    """Home page."""
    return render_template('index.html')


@app.route('/users')
def users():
    """List all users."""
    query = "SELECT id, username, email FROM users"
    db = get_db()
    cursor = db.cursor()
    cursor.execute(query)
    users = cursor.fetchall()
    return render_template('users.html', users=users)


@app.route('/add_user', methods=['GET', 'POST'])
def add_user():
    """Add a new user."""
    if request.method == 'POST':
        username = request.form['username']
        email = request.form['email']
        password = request.form['password']
        query = "INSERT INTO users (username, email, password) VALUES (?, ?, ?)"
        db = get_db()
        cursor = db.cursor()
        cursor.execute(query, (username, email, password))
```

```python
        db.commit()
        return redirect(url_for('users'))
    return render_template('add_user.html')


@app.route('/posts/<int:user_id>')
def posts(user_id):
    """List posts by a specific user."""
    query = "SELECT id, title, content, created_at FROM posts WHERE user_id = ?"
    db = get_db()
    cursor = db.cursor()
    cursor.execute(query, (user_id,))
    posts = cursor.fetchall()
    return render_template('posts.html', posts=posts, user_id=user_id)


@app.route('/add_post/<int:user_id>', methods=['GET', 'POST'])
def add_post(user_id):
    """Add a new post."""
    if request.method == 'POST':
        title = request.form['title']
        content = request.form['content']
        query = "INSERT INTO posts (user_id, title, content) VALUES (?, ?, ?)"
        db = get_db()
        cursor = db.cursor()
        cursor.execute(query, (user_id, title, content))
        db.commit()
        return redirect(url_for('posts', user_id=user_id))
    return render_template('add_post.html', user_id=user_id)
```

- **Templates:**
    - o Base Template (templates/base.html)

```
base.html ×
templates > base.html > ...
1   <!DOCTYPE html>
2   <html lang="en">
3   <head>
4       <meta charset="UTF-8">
5       <meta name="viewport" content="width=device-width, initial-scale=1.0">
6       <title>Blog Application</title>
7       <link rel="stylesheet" href="{{ url_for('static', filename='styles.css') }}">
8   </head>
9   <body>
10      <header>
11          <h1>Blog Application</h1>
12          <nav>
13              <a href="{{ url_for('index') }}">Home</a>
14              <a href="{{ url_for('users') }}">Users</a>
15          </nav>
16      </header>
17      <main>
18          {% block content %}{% endblock %}
19      </main>
20  </body>
21  </html>
```

- Home Page (templates/index.html)

```
base.html          index.html ×
templates > index.html > ...
1   {% extends 'base.html' %}
2
3   {% block content %}
4   <h2>Welcome to the Blog Application</h2>
5   <p>Use the navigation menu to manage users and posts.</p>
6   {% endblock %}
```

- List Users (templates/users.html)

```
base.html          index.html          users.html ×
templates > users.html > ...
1   {% extends 'base.html' %}
2
3   {% block content %}
4   <h2>Users</h2>
5   <a href="{{ url_for('add_user') }}">Add User</a>
6   <ul>
7       {% for user in users %}
8       <li>
9           {{ user.username }} ({{ user.email }}) -
10          <a href="{{ url_for('posts', user_id=user.id) }}">View Posts</a>
11      </li>
12      {% endfor %}
13  </ul>
14  {% endblock %}
```

- Add User (templates/add_user.html)

```
base.html      index.html      users.html      add_user.html  ×

templates > add_user.html > ...
1    {% extends 'base.html' %}
2
3    {% block content %}
4    <h2>Add User</h2>
5    <form method="POST">
6        <label>Username:</label>
7        <input type="text" name="username" required>
8        <label>Email:</label>
9        <input type="email" name="email" required>
10       <label>Password:</label>
11       <input type="password" name="password" required
12       <button type="submit">Add User</button>
13   </form>
14   {% endblock %}
```

- List Posts (templates/posts.html)

```
base.html      users.html      add_user.html      posts.html  ×

templates > posts.html > ...
1    {% extends 'base.html' %}
2
3    {% block content %}
4    <h2>Posts</h2>
5    <a href="{{ url_for('add_post', user_id=user_id) }}">Add Post</a>
6    <ul>
7        {% for post in posts %}
8        <li>
9            <strong>{{ post.title }}</strong>: {{ post.content }} ({{ post.created_at }})
10       </li>
11       {% endfor %}
12   </ul>
13   {% endblock %}
```

- Add Post (templates/add_post.html)

```
base.html      users.html      add_user.html      posts.html      add_post.html  ×

templates > add_post.html > ...
1    {% extends 'base.html' %}
2
3    {% block content %}
4    <h2>Add Post</h2>
5    <form method="POST">
6        <label>Title:</label>
7        <input type="text" name="title" required>
8        <label>Content:</label>
9        <textarea name="content" required></textarea>
10       <button type="submit">Add Post</button>
11   </form>
12   {% endblock %}
```

- **Static Files**
  - Create a static/styles.css file for basic styling:

```css
body {
    font-family: Arial, sans-serif;
    margin: 0;
    padding: 0;
    background-color: #f9f9f9;
}

header {
    background-color: #333;
    color: #fff;
    padding: 10px 20px;
}

header nav a {
    color: #fff;
    margin-right: 10px;
    text-decoration: none;
}

main {
    padding: 20px;
}
```

- **Run the Application**
  - Run the Flask app:

```
flask run
```

Visit the app at http://127.0.0.1:5000.

You now have a complete Flask blog application with SQLite and templates!

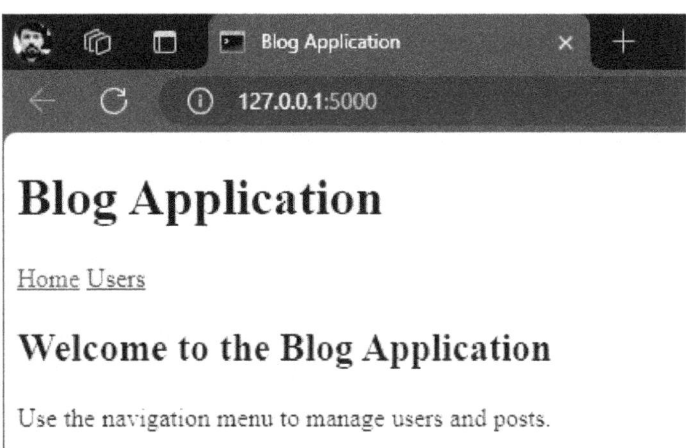
Blog Application
127.0.0.1:5000
Blog Application
Home Users
Welcome to the Blog Application
Use the navigation menu to manage users and posts.

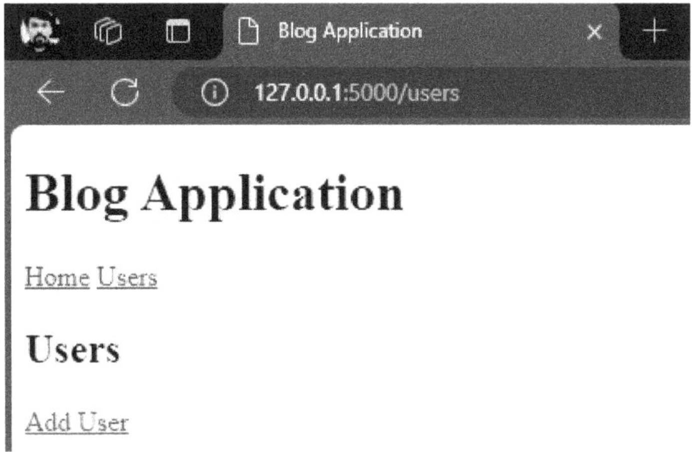
Blog Application
127.0.0.1:5000/users
Blog Application
Home Users
Users
Add User

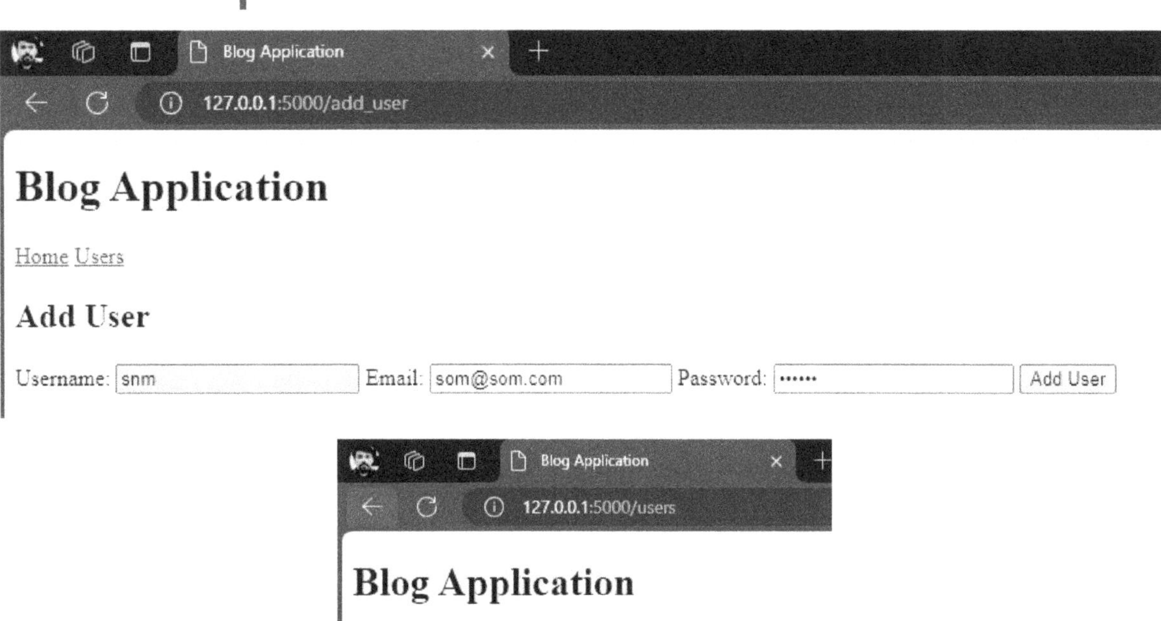
Blog Application
127.0.0.1:5000/add_user
Blog Application
Home Users
Add User
Username: snm    Email: som@som.com    Password: ••••••    Add User
Blog Application
127.0.0.1:5000/users
Blog Application
Home Users
Users
Add User
• snm (som@som.com) - View Posts

Blog Application
127.0.0.1:5000/posts/1
Blog Application
Home Users
Posts
Add Post

Blog Application
127.0.0.1:5000/add_post/1
Blog Application
Home Users
Add Post
This is a sample blog.
Title: A Sample Blog    Content:    Add Post

Blog Application
127.0.0.1:5000/posts/1
Blog Application
Home Users
Posts
Add Post
• A Sample Blog: This is a sample blog. (2024-12-31 07:31:42)

# 21. SQLAlchemy

**SQLAlchemy** is a powerful Python library that facilitates interaction with databases through an Object Relational Mapping (**ORM**) approach and direct SQL capabilities. It provides tools to work with relational databases in a way that combines the best of high-level abstraction and fine-grained control over SQL execution. Performing **CRUD** operations using raw SQL in Flask web applications can be cumbersome. To simplify this process, **SQLAlchemy**, a robust Python toolkit and **ORM**, provides developers with the full power and flexibility of SQL. Flask-SQLAlchemy, an extension for Flask, seamlessly integrates **SQLAlchemy** into Flask applications.

**SQLAlchemy** stands out as a robust and versatile tool for Python developers, enabling them to work efficiently with databases while maintaining flexibility and control.

## What is Object Relation Mapping (ORM)?

Programming language platforms are mostly object-oriented, whereas data in RDBMS servers is organized into tables. Object-Relational Mapping (ORM) is a technique used to align object attributes with the structure of database tables. An ORM API simplifies this process by providing methods for performing CRUD operations without the need to write raw SQL.

Key Features

- **ORM (Object Relational Mapping):**
    - Converts Python objects into database tables and vice versa.
    - Simplifies database manipulation by allowing developers to work with Python classes instead of SQL queries.
    - Enables relationships between tables using Python attributes.

- **Core (SQL Expression Language):**
    - A lower-level API for constructing and executing raw SQL queries.
    - Ideal for performance-critical tasks or when greater control over SQL is needed.

- **Flexibility:**
    - Works with a wide variety of databases, including SQLite, PostgreSQL, MySQL, Oracle, and more.
    - Easily switches between different database engines with minimal code changes.

- **Schema Definition and Migration:**
    - Supports schema definition via Python code using the declarative_base approach.
    - Integrates with migration tools like Alembic for evolving database schemas over time.

- **Connection Pooling:**
    - Manages connections efficiently to enhance application performance.

      o   Includes support for advanced connection strategies like pooling and lazy loading.

# Components of SQLAlchemy

- **Engine**:
    - o   Central object connecting SQLAlchemy to the database.
    - o   Responsible for managing connections and issuing SQL commands.
- **Session**:
    - o   Handles transactions and ensures objects are synchronized with the database.
    - o   Acts as a staging zone for changes to the database.
- **Declarative Base**:
    - o   A foundational class for defining mapped classes and tables.
    - o   Simplifies ORM by combining table and class definitions into a single structure.
- **Query**:
    - o   Provides methods for retrieving records from the database.
    - o   Supports filtering, joining, and chaining of query operations.
- **Metadata**:
    - o   Contains a catalog of tables and their definitions.
    - o   Can be used independently of the ORM for advanced SQL expression use.

# Setting Up SQLAlchemy

- Before diving into examples, install SQLAlchemy using pip: `pip install sqlalchemy`

# Example Usage

- **ORM Example**:

```python
from sqlalchemy import create_engine
from sqlalchemy.ext.declarative import declarative_base
from sqlalchemy import Column, Integer, String
from sqlalchemy.orm import sessionmaker

# Define database engine
engine = create_engine('sqlite:///example.db')
```

```python
# Define base class
Base = declarative_base()

# Define a table as a class
class User(Base):
    __tablename__ = 'users'
    id = Column(Integer, primary_key=True)
    name = Column(String)
    age = Column(Integer)

# Create tables
Base.metadata.create_all(engine)

# Create a session
Session = sessionmaker(bind=engine)
session = Session()

# Add a new user
new_user = User(name='Alice', age=30)
session.add(new_user)
session.commit()

# Query users
users = session.query(User).all()
for user in users:
    print(user.name)
```

- **SQL Expression Language Example:**

```python
from sqlalchemy import create_engine, Table, Column, Integer, String, MetaData

# Define engine and metadata
engine = create_engine('sqlite:///example.db')
metadata = MetaData()

# Define a table
users = Table('users', metadata,
              Column('id', Integer, primary_key=True),
              Column('name', String),
              Column('age', Integer))
```

```python
# Create table
metadata.create_all(engine)

# Insert data
with engine.connect() as conn:
    conn.execute(users.insert(), {"name": "Bob", "age": 25})

# Query data
with engine.connect() as conn:
    result = conn.execute(users.select())
    for row in result:
        print(row)
```

# Best Practices

- **Use Connection Pooling**:

  - Leverage built-in pooling to manage database connections effectively in high-load applications.

- **Follow SQLAlchemy Conventions**:

  - Stick to naming conventions and practices for maintainability and consistency.

- **Optimize Queries**:

  - Use lazy loading and eager loading appropriately to avoid unnecessary database hits.

- **Use Alembic for Migrations**:

  - Manage schema changes systematically in production environments.

- **Test with Multiple Databases**:

  - Ensure compatibility across different database systems if portability is required.

# Common Challenges

- **Performance Overhead**:

  - ORM can add overhead compared to raw SQL in highly performance-sensitive applications.

- **Steep Learning Curve**:

  - SQLAlchemy's depth and flexibility can be intimidating for beginners.

- **Migration Complexity**:

  - Evolving schemas in a live application requires careful planning and tools like Alembic.

# Examples

**Example 1: ORM Basics**

- Setting Up a Database and Table:

```python
from sqlalchemy import create_engine
from sqlalchemy.ext.declarative import declarative_base
from sqlalchemy import Column, Integer, String
from sqlalchemy.orm import sessionmaker

# Step 1: Create a database engine
engine = create_engine('sqlite:///example.db')  # SQLite database

# Step 2: Define a base class using the ORM
Base = declarative_base()

# Step 3: Define a table as a Python class
class User(Base):
    __tablename__ = 'users'
    id = Column(Integer, primary_key=True)
    name = Column(String, nullable=False)
    age = Column(Integer)

# Step 4: Create the table in the database
Base.metadata.create_all(engine)
```

- Adding Records:

```python
# Step 5: Create a session to interact with the database
Session = sessionmaker(bind=engine)
session = Session()

# Step 6: Add a new user
new_user = User(name="Alice", age=25)
session.add(new_user)
session.commit()

print("User added successfully!")
```

- Querying Records:

```python
# Fetch all users
users = session.query(User).all()
for user in users:
    print(f"ID: {user.id}, Name: {user.name}, Age: {user.age}")

# Fetch a specific user by filtering
user = session.query(User).filter_by(name="Alice").first()
if user:
    print(f"Found user: {user.name}, Age: {user.age}")
```

- Updating Records:

```python
# Update Alice's age
user.age = 26
session.commit()
print("User updated successfully!")
```

- Deleting Records:

```python
# Delete a user
session.delete(user)
session.commit()
print("User deleted successfully!")
```
-

## Example 2: Relationships Between Tables:

- Setting Up a One-to-Many Relationship

```python
from sqlalchemy import ForeignKey
from sqlalchemy.orm import relationship

class Post(Base):
    __tablename__ = 'posts'
    id = Column(Integer, primary_key=True)
    title = Column(String, nullable=False)
    content = Column(String)
    user_id = Column(Integer, ForeignKey('users.id'))

    # Define relationship with the User table
    user = relationship("User", back_populates="posts")

# Add the reverse relationship in the User class
User.posts = relationship("Post", order_by=Post.id, back_populates="user")

# Create tables
Base.metadata.create_all(engine)
```

- Adding Related Records

```python
# Create tables
Base.metadata.create_all(engine)

# Create a user and their posts
user = User(name="Bob", age=30)
post1 = Post(title="First Post", content="Hello, world!", user=user)
post2 = Post(title="Second Post", content="SQLAlchemy is great!", user=user)

# Add and commit the records
session.add(user)
session.add(post1)
session.add(post2)
session.commit()

print("User and posts added successfully!")
```

- Querying Related Records

```python
# Fetch user and their posts
user = session.query(User).filter_by(name="Bob").first()
print(f"User: {user.name}, Age: {user.age}")
for post in user.posts:
    print(f"Post: {post.title}, Content: {post.content}")
```

**Example 3: Using the Core API**

- Defining Tables Programmatically:

```python
from sqlalchemy import MetaData, Table, Column, Integer, String

# Define metadata
metadata = MetaData()

# Define a table
tasks = Table(
    'tasks', metadata,
    Column('id', Integer, primary_key=True),
    Column('description', String, nullable=False),
    Column('completed', Integer, default=0)
)

# Create the table in the database
metadata.create_all(engine)
```

- Inserting Data

```python
with engine.connect() as conn:
    conn.execute(tasks.insert().values(description="Learn SQLAlchemy", completed=0))
    conn.execute(tasks.insert().values(description="Build a project", completed=0))
print("Tasks added!")
```

- Querying Data

```python
with engine.connect() as conn:
    result = conn.execute(tasks.select())
    for row in result:
        print(f"Task ID: {row.id}, Description: {row.description}, Completed: {row.completed}")
```

**Example 4: Connection Pooling**

- This ensures efficient management of database connections, especially for web applications with high traffic.

```python
from sqlalchemy.pool import QueuePool

# Create an engine with connection pooling
engine = create_engine(
    'sqlite:///example.db',
    poolclass=QueuePool,
    pool_size=5,
    max_overflow=10,
    pool_timeout=30
)
```

SQLAlchemy's flexibility allows developers to build scalable and maintainable applications, whether working on small projects with simple requirements or enterprise-grade systems requiring complex data relationships.

# Example Application:

Let us create an example of a complete Flask application that uses **SQLAlchemy** for database management, along with a template for rendering data. This application demonstrates how to perform **CRUD** (Create, Read, Update, Delete) operations and display results using an **HTML** template.

- Project Structure (Directory Structure):

```
flask_sqlalchemy_app/
├── app.py
├── models.py
├── templates/
│   ├── base.html
│   ├── index.html
│   ├── edit.html
├── static/
│   ├── style.css
├── requirements.txt
```

- requirements.txt

```
 requirements.txt  ×
 requirements.txt
1    flask
2    flask-sqlalchemy
3    flask-wtf
4    wtforms
5
```

```
pip install -r requirements.txt
```

This pip command will install all the required libraries for this project.

- **Application**: app.py

```python
from flask import Flask, render_template, request, redirect, url_for
from models import db, User


app = Flask(__name__)
app.config['SQLALCHEMY_DATABASE_URI'] = 'sqlite:///users.db'
app.config['SECRET_KEY'] = 'your_secret_key'


# Initialize the database
db.init_app(app)

# Create tables before handling requests
with app.app_context():
    db.create_all()


@app.route('/')
def index():
    users = User.query.all()
    return render_template('index.html', users=users)


@app.route('/add', methods=['POST'])
def add_user():
    name = request.form['name']
    age = request.form['age']
    new_user = User(name=name, age=int(age))
    db.session.add(new_user)
    db.session.commit()
    return redirect(url_for('index'))


@app.route('/edit/<int:user_id>', methods=['GET', 'POST'])
def edit_user(user_id):
```

```python
        user = User.query.get_or_404(user_id)
        if request.method == 'POST':
            user.name = request.form['name']
            user.age = int(request.form['age'])
            db.session.commit()
            return redirect(url_for('index'))
        return render_template('edit.html', user=user)


    @app.route('/delete/<int:user_id>')
    def delete_user(user_id):
        user = User.query.get_or_404(user_id)
        db.session.delete(user)
        db.session.commit()
        return redirect(url_for('index'))


    if __name__ == '__main__':
app.run(debug=True)
```

- **Model**: models.py

```python
models.py ×

models.py > ...
  1    from flask_sqlalchemy import SQLAlchemy
  2
  3    db = SQLAlchemy()
  4
  5    class User(db.Model):
  6        id = db.Column(db.Integer, primary_key=True)
  7        name = db.Column(db.String(80), nullable=False)
  8        age = db.Column(db.Integer, nullable=False)
```

- **Templates**:

  o   templates/base.html:

```
models.py        <> base.html  ×
templates > <> base.html > ...
    1   <!DOCTYPE html>
    2   <html lang="en">
    3   <head>
    4       <meta charset="UTF-8">
    5       <meta name="viewport" content="width=device-width, initial-scale=1.0">
    6       <title>User Management</title>
    7       <link rel="stylesheet" href="{{ url_for('static', filename='style.css') }}">
    8   </head>
    9   <body>
   10       <div class="container">
   11           <h1>User Management App</h1>
   12           {% block content %}{% endblock %}
   13       </div>
   14   </body>
   15   </html>
```

o   templates/index.html:

```
{% extends 'base.html' %}

{% block content %}
    <form action="/add" method="post">
        <input type="text" name="name" placeholder="Name" required>
        <input type="number" name="age" placeholder="Age" required>
        <button type="submit">Add User</button>
    </form>

    <table>
        <thead>
            <tr>
                <th>ID</th>
                <th>Name</th>
                <th>Age</th>
                <th>Actions</th>
            </tr>
        </thead>
        <tbody>
            {% for user in users %}
                <tr>
                    <td>{{ user.id }}</td>
                    <td>{{ user.name }}</td>
                    <td>{{ user.age }}</td>
                    <td>
                        <a href="/edit/{{ user.id }}">Edit</a>
```

```
                        <a href="/delete/{{ user.id }}" onclick="return confirm('Are
you sure?');">Delete</a>
                    </td>
                </tr>
            {% endfor %}
        </tbody>
    </table>
{% endblock %}
```

- o templates/edit.html

```
 models.py        <> base.html        <> index.html        <> edit.html   ×
templates > <> edit.html > ...
    1    {% extends 'base.html' %}
    2
    3    {% block content %}
    4        <form action="" method="post">
    5            <input type="text" name="name" value="{{ user.name }}" required>
    6            <input type="number" name="age" value="{{ user.age }}" required>
    7            <button type="submit">Update User</button>
    8        </form>
    9    {% endblock %}
```

- static/style.css

```css
body {
  font-family: Arial, sans-serif;
  margin: 0;
  padding: 0;
  background-color: #f4f4f9;
}

.container {
  width: 80%;
  margin: 20px auto;
  background: white;
  padding: 20px;
  border-radius: 8px;
  box-shadow: 0 0 10px rgba(0, 0, 0, 0.1);
}

h1 {
  text-align: center;
  margin-bottom: 20px;
```

```css
}

form {
  margin-bottom: 20px;
}

input[type="text"], input[type="number"] {
  padding: 10px;
  margin-right: 10px;
  border: 1px solid #ccc;
  border-radius: 4px;
}

button {
  padding: 10px 15px;
  background-color: #007bff;
  color: white;
  border: none;
  border-radius: 4px;
  cursor: pointer;
}

table {
  width: 100%;
  border-collapse: collapse;
}

table th, table td {
  border: 1px solid #ddd;
  padding: 10px;
  text-align: left;
}

table th {
  background-color: #007bff;
  color: white;
}
```

- Running the Application
  - o Run the application:

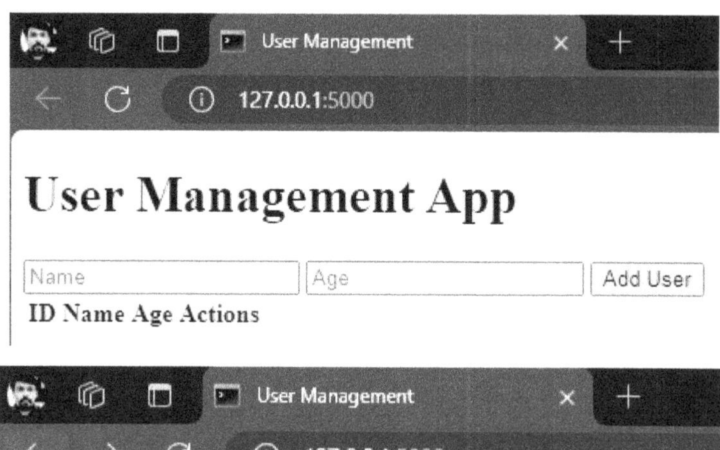
User Management
127.0.0.1:5000
User Management App
Name
Age
Add User
ID Name Age Actions

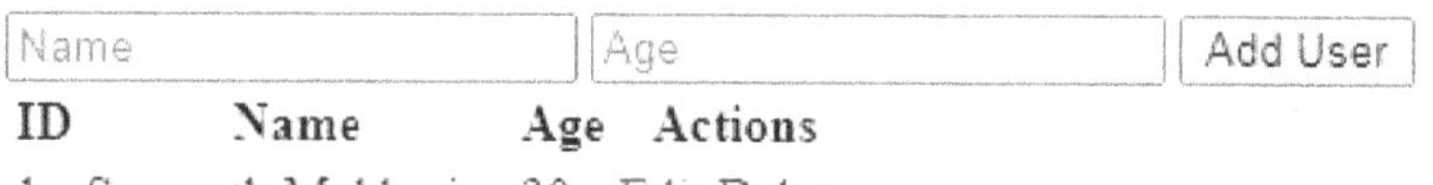
User Management
127.0.0.1:5000
User Management App
Name
Age
Add User
ID        Name        Age   Actions
1    Somnath Mukherjee 30    Edit Delete

User Management
127.0.0.1:5000/edit/1
User Management App
Somnath Mukherjee
30
Update User

# 22. Flask-SocketIO

Flask-SocketIO is an extension for Flask that enables the use of WebSockets and other asynchronous protocols for real-time communication. It is built on top of the Socket.IO protocol, allowing for bidirectional communication between the server and clients.

- **WebSocket Basics:**

  - WebSockets are a protocol for full-duplex communication channels over a single TCP connection. They allow servers and clients to send messages to each other without the need for the client to continuously poll the server.

  - Unlike the standard HTTP request-response model, WebSocket communication persists, making it ideal for real-time applications like chat apps, notifications, live updates, and multiplayer games.

- **Flask-SocketIO Overview:**

  - Flask-SocketIO adds WebSocket functionality to a Flask application. It wraps around the Socket.IO JavaScript library and provides an easy-to-use interface for Python developers to manage WebSockets and other communication features.

  - It is an asynchronous framework that uses a background thread for managing WebSocket connections, making it efficient for real-time updates.

Flask-SocketIO is a powerful extension that adds real-time, bidirectional communication to Flask applications. By leveraging WebSockets, it enables the development of interactive applications that require live updates, such as chat rooms, games, and live notifications. With the ability to handle multiple clients simultaneously using asynchronous programming libraries like Eventlet or gevent, Flask-SocketIO is an excellent choice for building scalable and responsive web applications.

## Key Features of Flask-SocketIO

- **Real-Time Communication:**

  - Flask-SocketIO allows real-time communication between the client (usually a browser) and the server. This is essential for applications that require live updates, such as:

    - **Chat Applications:** Real-time messaging between users.

    - **Live Data Feeds:** Instant updates for stock prices, sports scores, etc.

    - **Games:** Real-time multiplayer interactions.

    - **Collaborative Apps:** Collaborative editing or real-time notifications.

- **Events and Event Handling:**

  - Event-driven programming is a core concept in Flask-SocketIO. Events are emitted from both the server and the client.

- o On the server side, you use decorators to listen to specific events and handle them. These events can be custom defined.

```python
from flask import Flask
from flask_socketio import SocketIO, emit

# Initialize Flask app and SocketIO
app = Flask(__name__)
app.config['SECRET_KEY'] = 'your_secret_key'
socketio = SocketIO(app)

@socketio.on('message')
def handle_message(message):
    print(f"Message received: {message}")
    emit('message', 'Response from server')
```

- o In the example above:

  - The @socketio.on('message') decorator listens for the message event sent from the client.

  - The handle_message function is triggered when the event is received and sends a response back to the client using the emit function.

- **Emit and Broadcast:**

  - o emit() is used to send a message from the server to the client.

  - o broadcast allows you to send messages to all clients except the sender.

```python
emit('message', 'This message is for all clients', broadcast=True)
```

- **Namespaces:**

  - o A namespace allows you to separate different channels of communication. By default, all events are emitted on the '/' namespace, but you can create custom namespaces.

```python
@socketio.on('my_event', namespace='/chat')
def handle_chat_event(message):
    print(f"Message in chat: {message}")
```

  - o In the above code, the event my_event is specific to the /chat namespace. Clients would have to connect to this namespace to receive or send events.

- **Rooms:**

  - o A room is a group of clients that can receive messages together. Clients can join and leave rooms dynamically.

- o Rooms are useful when you want to send messages to a specific group of users (e.g., chat rooms in a messaging app).

```python
@socketio.on('join')
def join_room(data):
    join_room(data['room'])
    emit('message', f"Joined {data['room']}")


@socketio.on('leave')
def leave_room(data):
    leave_room(data['room'])
    emit('message', f"Left {data['room']}")
```

- o The join_room and leave_room functions are used to manage which room a client belongs to, and messages can be sent to a room by emitting to it:

```python
emit('message', 'Hello everyone in the room', room='room_name')
```

- **Broadcasting:**

  - o Broadcasting means sending a message to all connected clients or clients within a specific room. This is useful for notifications and live updates.

  - o In Flask-SocketIO, you can broadcast a message like this:

```python
emit('message', 'This is broadcasted to everyone', broadcast=True)
```

  - o You can also broadcast to rooms specifically.

- **SocketIO Client Integration**

  - o On the client side, you need the Socket.IO JavaScript library to communicate with the Flask-SocketIO server.

  - o The client can emit events and listen to server-side messages.

```javascript
const socket = io();

// Emit an event to the server
socket.emit('message', 'Hello from the client');

// Listen for messages from the server
socket.on('message', function(data) {
    console.log('Message from server:', data);
});
```

- **Flask-SocketIO with AsyncIO and Eventlet:**

  - Flask-SocketIO uses asynchronous frameworks like Eventlet, gevent, or asyncio for handling concurrent connections. This allows Flask to support long-lived WebSocket connections.

    - **Eventlet**: A popular networking library for Python that uses green threads to handle multiple tasks simultaneously. It is used to provide concurrency without the complexity of threads.

    - **gevent**: Another concurrency library that works with greenlets to provide similar functionality as Eventlet.

    - **asyncio**: For Python 3.7+, Flask-SocketIO can also use the native asyncio library for concurrency.

  - Example for running with Eventlet:

    ```python
    from eventlet import monkey_patch
    monkey_patch()  # Patch standard library for cooperative multitasking

    socketio.run(app)
    ```

- **Error Handling:**

  - SocketIO provides mechanisms to handle errors in communication.

  - You can use decorators like @socketio.on_error() to define custom error handling for events.

    ```python
    @socketio.on_error()  # Global error handler
    def error_handler(error):
        print(f"An error occurred: {error}")
    ```

# Practical Uses of Flask–SocketIO

- **Chat Applications**

  - Flask-SocketIO is often used to build real-time chat systems where users can send and receive messages instantly.

- **Real-Time Dashboards**

  - Web applications like dashboards that display live updates from a backend system (e.g., stock prices, social media feed) can utilize Flask-SocketIO.

- **Gaming and Multiplayer Applications**

  - Flask-SocketIO is ideal for building multiplayer games where game state updates must be sent in real-time to players.

- **Collaborative Applications**

- o Any app where multiple users interact with shared data (e.g., collaborative document editing, whiteboards) benefits from Flask-SocketIO.

- **Live Notifications**

  - o Flask-SocketIO can handle push notifications, letting your web application send updates to users when certain events happen on the server.

Key Flask-SocketIO Methods and Functions

- **emit(event, data, broadcast=False, room=None):** Sends an event with associated data to clients. Use broadcast=True to send to all clients, or room to send to a specific room.

- **join_room(room):** Adds the current client to a specified room.

- **leave_room(room):** Removes the client from the specified room.

- **send(message, broadcast=False):** Sends a simple text message to the client.

- **on_event(event_name):** Decorator for handling events.

Example Application:

An application demonstrates a real-time chat application.

- **Directory Structure**

```
flask_socketio_project/
|
├── app/
|   ├── __init__.py
|   ├── routes.py
|   ├── events.py
|   ├──templates/
|       ├── index.html
|
├── static/
|   ├── css/
|   |   └── styles.css
|
├── .venv/
|
├── requirements.txt
└── run.py
```

- **requirements.txt**

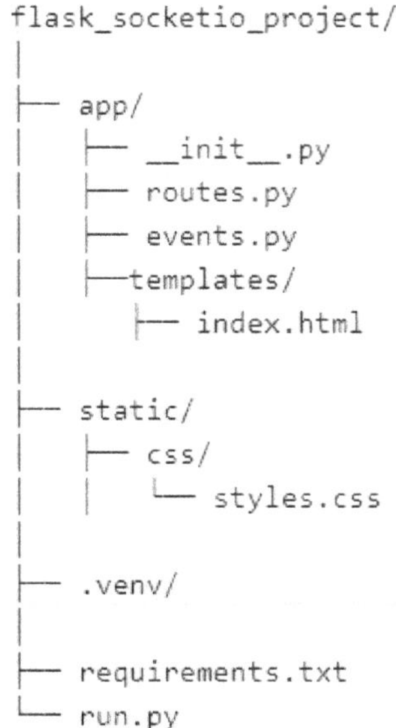

```
requirements.txt  ×

requirements.txt
1    Flask==2.3.2
2    Flask-SocketIO==5.3.3
3    eventlet==0.33.3
4
```

- **app/__init__.py**

```
from flask import Flask
from flask_socketio import SocketIO

# Initialize Flask app and SocketIO
app = Flask(__name__)
app.config['SECRET_KEY'] = 'your_secret_key'
socketio = SocketIO(app)

from app import routes, events
```

- **app/routes.py**

```
from app import app
from flask import render_template

@app.route('/')
def index():
    return render_template('index.html')
```

- **app/events.py**

```
from app import socketio
from flask_socketio import emit

@socketio.on('message')
def handle_message(data):
    print(f"Message received: {data}")
    emit('message', f"Server received: {data}", broadcast=True)
```

- **templates/index.html**

```
<!DOCTYPE html>
<html lang="en">
```

```html
<head>
    <meta charset="UTF-8">
    <meta name="viewport" content="width=device-width, initial-scale=1.0">
    <title>Flask-SocketIO Chat</title>
    <link rel="stylesheet" href="/static/css/styles.css">
</head>
<body>
    <h1>Flask-SocketIO Chat</h1>
    <div id="chat">
        <ul id="messages"></ul>
        <input id="messageInput" type="text" placeholder="Type a message...">
        <button id="sendBtn">Send</button>
    </div>
    <script src="https://cdn.socket.io/4.5.0/socket.io.min.js"></script>
    <script>
        const socket = io();
        const sendBtn = document.getElementById('sendBtn');
        const messageInput = document.getElementById('messageInput');
        const messages = document.getElementById('messages');

        sendBtn.addEventListener('click', () => {
            const message = messageInput.value;
            socket.emit('message', message);
            messageInput.value = '';
        });

        socket.on('message', (data) => {
            const newMessage = document.createElement('li');
            newMessage.textContent = data;
            messages.appendChild(newMessage);
        });
    </script>
</body>
</html>
```

- **static/css/styles.css**

```
# styles.css   ×

static > css > # styles.css > ...
   1   body {
   2       font-family: Arial, sans-serif;
   3       margin: 0;
   4       padding: 20px;
   5       background-color: ☐#f0f0f0;
   6   }
   7
   8   #chat {
   9       margin-top: 20px;
  10   }
  11
  12   #messages {
  13       list-style-type: none;
  14       padding: 0;
  15   }
  16
  17   #messages li {
  18       padding: 8px;
  19       margin-bottom: 5px;
  20       background-color: ☐#e0e0e0;
  21       border-radius: 5px;
  22   }
```

- **run.py**

```
# styles.css        🍂 socket001.py        🍂 run.py        ×

🍂 run.py
   1   from app import app, socketio
   2
   3   if __name__ == '__main__':
   4       socketio.run(app, debug=True)
   5
```

- Install dependencies:
  - pip install -r requirements.txt

- python run.py

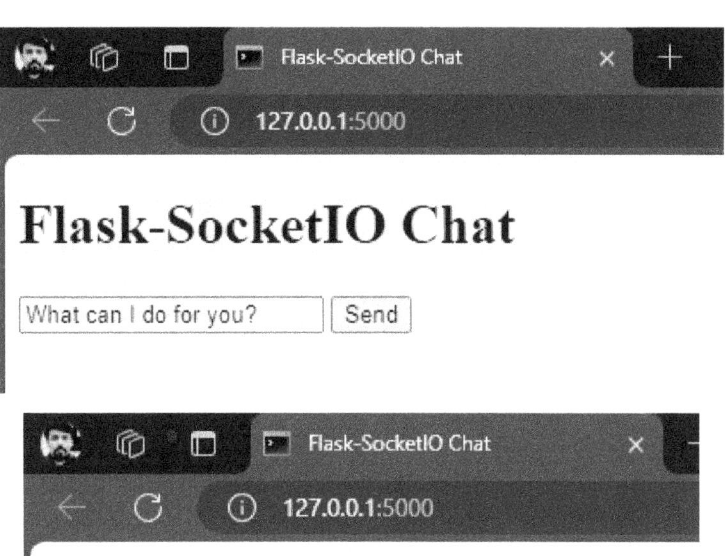

Flask-SocketIO Chat
127.0.0.1:5000
Flask-SocketIO Chat
What can I do for you?    Send
Flask-SocketIO Chat
127.0.0.1:5000
Flask-SocketIO Chat
Server received: What can I do for you?
Tell me about the weather    Send

# 23. Flask-Restful

Flask-RESTful is an extension for Flask that simplifies building RESTful APIs. It provides tools and utilities for creating APIs quickly, with less boilerplate code.

## Core Concepts

- **Resources**

    o In Flask-RESTful, API endpoints are represented as "resources." A resource corresponds to an entity in your application, such as a user, book, or task.

- **Routes**

    o Resources are mapped to URLs using routes. Flask-RESTful simplifies routing with a Resource class.

- **HTTP Methods**

    o RESTful APIs use HTTP methods to perform CRUD operations:

        ▪ GET: Retrieve data.

        ▪ POST: Create new data.

        ▪ PUT: Update existing data.

        ▪ DELETE: Remove data.

- **Request Parsing**

    o Flask-RESTful provides *reqparse* to handle and validate incoming request parameters.

- **Error Handling**

    o Custom error handling is easy to implement for API responses.

## Installation

```
pip install flask-restful
```

- **Simple Example:**

```python
from flask import Flask
from flask_restful import Resource, Api


# Step 1: Initialize the Flask application and Flask-RESTful API
app = Flask(__name__)
api = Api(app)


# Step 2: Define a Resource
```

```
class HelloWorld(Resource):
    def get(self):
        return {"message": "Hello, World!"}


# Step 3: Add the Resource to the API
api.add_resource(HelloWorld, "/")


# Step 4: Run the Flask application
if __name__ == "__main__":
    app.run(debug=True)
```

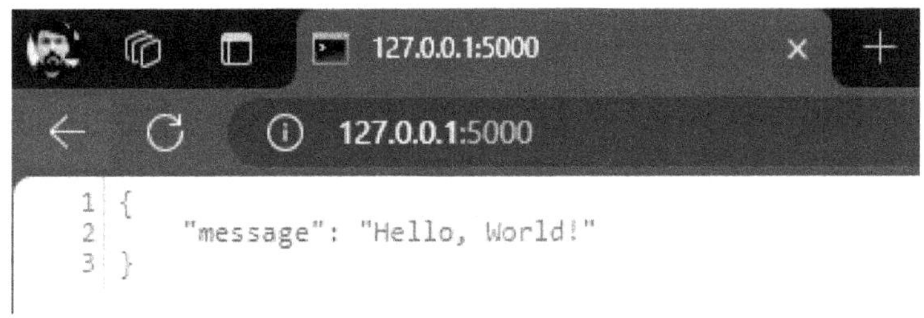


- **Explanation**

  o **Step 1**: Initialize the Flask Application and Flask-RESTful API

  ```
  app = Flask(__name__)   # Create an instance of the Flask class.
  api = Api(app)          # Bind the Flask app to the Flask-RESTful API.
  ```

    - app = Flask(__name__): Creates the Flask application instance.

    - api = Api(app): Wraps the Flask app with the Flask-RESTful Api class, allowing the creation of RESTful APIs.

  o **Step 2**: Define a Resource

  ```
  class HelloWorld(Resource):
      def get(self):
          return {"message": "Hello, World!"}
  ```

    - **Resource**: A class representing an API endpoint. In this case, HelloWorld represents the root (/) endpoint.

    - **Method**: Defines what should happen for a specific HTTP method (e.g., GET).

    - **get(self)**: Handles GET requests to return a JSON response {"message": "Hello, World!"}.

  o **Step 3**: Add the Resource to the API

  ```
  api.add_resource(HelloWorld, "/")
  ```

- **add_resource**: Maps the resource (HelloWorld) to a specific route (/).

  - **HelloWorld**: The class that defines the resource.

  - **"/"**: The URL route where this resource is accessible (in this case, the root).

  - **Step 4**: Run the Flask Application

```python
if __name__ == "__main__":
    app.run(debug=True)
```

  - **app.run(debug=True)**: Starts the Flask development server. The debug=True flag enables automatic reloads and detailed error messages during development.

- **How It Works**

  - When you run the script, the Flask application starts with a web server.

  - Accessing http://127.0.0.1:5000/ in a browser or API tool (like Postman) sends a GET request to the root endpoint (/).

  - The get method in the HelloWorld resource handles the request and returns the JSON response {"message": "Hello, World!"}.

- **Key Takeaways**

  - Flask-RESTful simplifies defining resources and routes.

  - Each Resource class corresponds to a set of endpoints.

  - Use api.add_resource to map resources to routes.

  - JSON responses are straightforward with Python dictionaries.

# CRUD Example with Flask-RESTful

- Create

- Retrieve

- Update

- Delete

**The Application File:**

```python
from flask import Flask, request
from flask_restful import Resource, Api


app = Flask(__name__)
api = Api(app)
```

```python
# In-memory database
books = {
    "1": {"title": "Hounds of Baskerville", "author": "Sir Arthur Conan Doyle"},
    "2": {"title": "Les Misérables", "author": "Victor Hugo"},
}


# Resource for individual books
class Book(Resource):
    def get(self, book_id):
        if book_id not in books:
            return {"message": "Book not found"}, 404
        return {book_id: books[book_id]}

    def put(self, book_id):
        data = request.json
        if not data or "title" not in data or "author" not in data:
            return {"message": "Missing 'title' or 'author'"}, 400
        books[book_id] = {"title": data["title"], "author": data["author"]}
        return {book_id: books[book_id]}, 201

    def delete(self, book_id):
        if book_id in books:
            del books[book_id]
            return {"message": "Book deleted successfully"}
        return {"message": "Book not found"}, 404

# Resource for the collection of books
class BookList(Resource):
    def get(self):
        return books

    def post(self):
        data = request.json
        if not data or "title" not in data or "author" not in data:
            return {"message": "Missing 'title' or 'author'"}, 400
        book_id = str(len(books) + 1)
        books[book_id] = {"title": data["title"], "author": data["author"]}
        return {book_id: books[book_id]}, 201


# Add resources to the API
api.add_resource(Book, "/books/<string:book_id>")
```

```python
api.add_resource(BookList, "/books")


if __name__ == "__main__":
    app.run(debug=True)
```

```
1  {
2      "1": {
3          "title": "Hounds of Baskerville",
4          "author": "Sir Arthur Conan Doyle"
5      },
6      "2": {
7          "title": "Les Misérables",
8          "author": "Victor Hugo"
9      }
10 }
```

```
1  {
2      "2": {
3          "title": "Les Misérables",
4          "author": "Victor Hugo"
5      }
6  }
```

Explanation:

- **Step 1:** Flask App and Flask-RESTful Initialization

```python
app = Flask(__name__)
api = Api(app)
```

  - Initializes the Flask application and binds it to Flask-RESTful's Api.

- **Step 2:** In-Memory Database

```python
# In-memory database
books = {
    "1": {"title": "Hounds of Baskerville", "author": "Sir Arthur Conan Doyle"},
    "2": {"title": "Les Misérables", "author": "Victor Hugo"},
}
```

  - A dictionary simulates a database. Keys are book IDs, and values are book details.

- **Individual Book Resource:** Book

- o Handles operations for a single book (/books/<book_id>).

  - GET Method

```
def get(self, book_id):
    if book_id not in books:
        return {"message": "Book not found"}, 404
    return {book_id: books[book_id]}
```

    - o Retrieves a book by its ID.

    - o Returns 404 if the book is not found.

  - PUT Method

```
def put(self, book_id):
    data = request.json
    if not data or "title" not in data or "author" not in data:
        return {"message": "Missing 'title' or 'author'"}, 400
    books[book_id] = {"title": data["title"], "author": data["author"]}
    return {book_id: books[book_id]}, 201
```

    - o Updates or creates a book by its ID.

    - o If the book exists, updates its details. Otherwise, create a new book.

  - DELETE Method

```
def delete(self, book_id):
    if book_id in books:
        del books[book_id]
        return {"message": "Book deleted successfully"}
    return {"message": "Book not found"}, 404
```

    - o Deletes a book by its ID.

    - o Returns 404 if the book does not exist.

- o **Collection Resource**: BookList

  - Handles operations for all books (/books).

  - GET Method

```
def get(self):
    return books
```

    - Retrieves all books in the "database".

  - POST Method

```
def post(self):
    data = request.json
    if not data or "title" not in data or "author" not in data:
        return {"message": "Missing 'title' or 'author'"}, 400
    book_id = str(len(books) + 1)
    books[book_id] = {"title": data["title"], "author": data["author"]}
    return {book_id: books[book_id]}, 201
```

- Adds a new book to the collection.

- Assign a new ID to the book and add it to the books dictionary.

o **Routes:**

- /books

  - GET: Fetch all books.

  - POST: Add a new book.

- /books/<book_id>

  - GET: Fetch a book by its ID.

  - PUT: Update or create a book by its ID.

  - DELETE: Delete a book with its ID.

o **How to Test:**

- Use Postman, cURL, or any other tool for API testing.

- Examples:

  - Retrieve All Books

    o Request: GET /books

    o Response: Postman

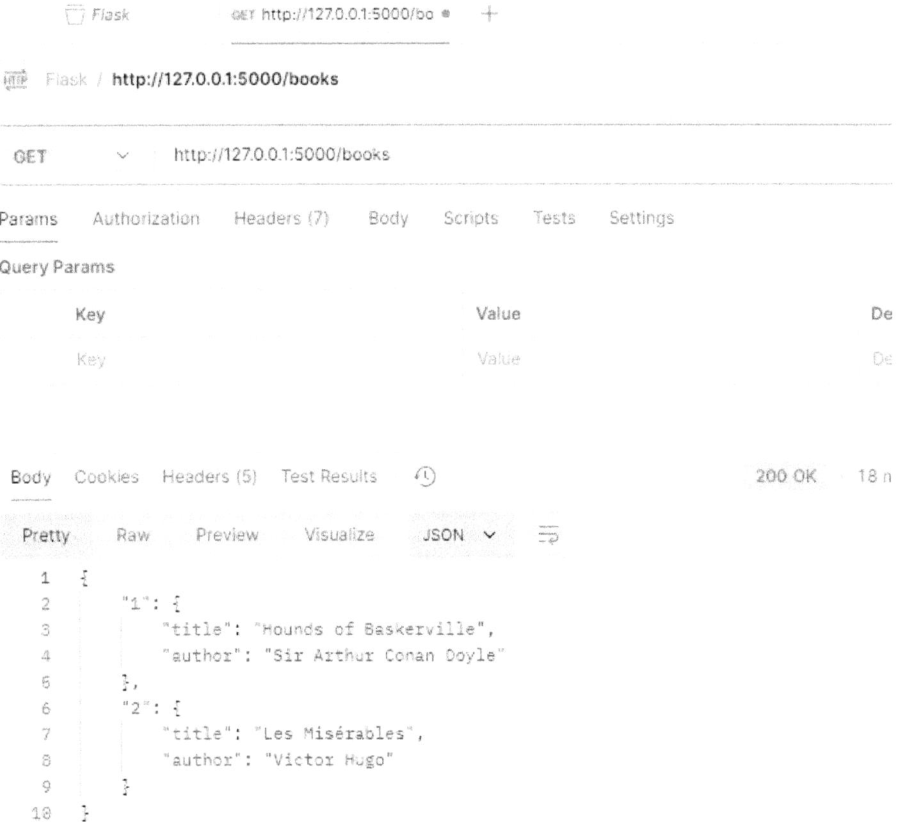



- Retrieving a Book

  o Request: GET /books/1

  o Response

- Add a New Book

- o Request: POST /books

- **Update a Book**

  - o Request: PUT /books/2

- **Delete a Book**
- **Request: DELETE /books/1**
- **Response:**

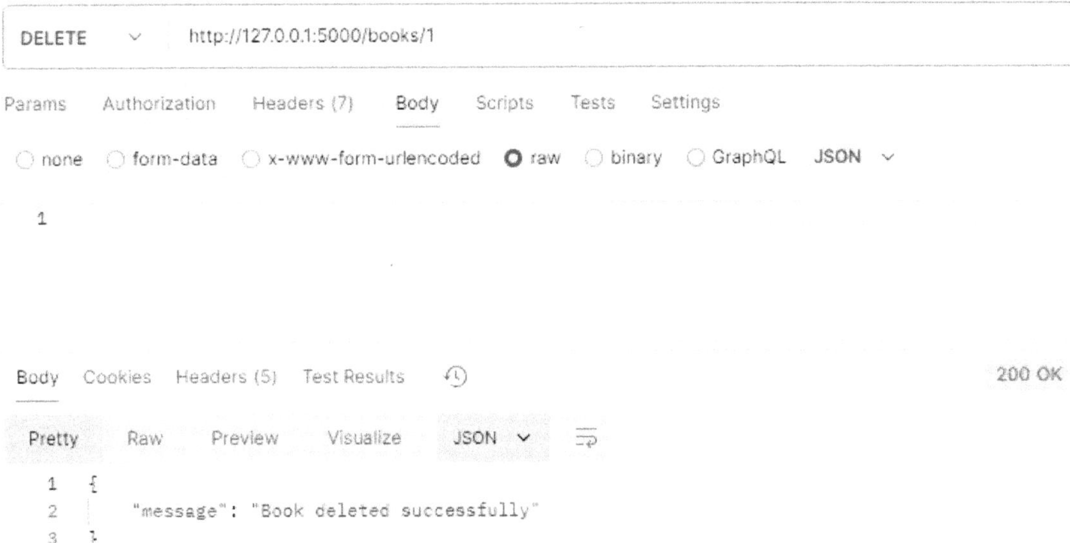

# 24. Testing

Testing in Flask is essential to ensure that your web application behaves as expected. Flask provides robust tools and practices for testing, allowing developers to write unit tests, integration tests, and end-to-end tests.

## Types of Testing

- **Unit Testing**

    o Focuses on individual components of your application, such as functions, routes, or services.

- **Integration Testing**

    o Ensure that different components of the application work together correctly.

- **End-to-End Testing**

    o Simulates real-world scenarios by testing the application from start to finish, often using tools like Selenium or Playwright.

## Tools and Libraries

- **unittest**: Python's built-in library for testing.

- **pytest**: A more powerful and feature-rich testing framework.

- **Flask-Testing**: An extension for testing Flask applications.

- **pytest-flask**: A pytest plugin for simplifying Flask application tests.

- **Mocking Libraries**: Tools like unittest.mock or responses for simulating external dependencies.

## Installation:

- pip install pytest coverage

- This will install both the pytest and coverage.

## Setting Up a Test Environment

- Flask provides a built-in testing mode that can be activated using:

```python
app.config['TESTING'] = True
app.config['DEBUG'] = False
```

- Why TESTING Mode?

- o It ensures error handling is strict.

- o Prevents live emails, database writes, or other unintended side effects.

# Writing Tests in Flask

- **Creating a Test Client**

    - o Flask's test client allows you to simulate requests to your application without starting a server:

```python
from flask import Flask
import unittest


app = Flask(__name__)


@app.route('/')
def home():
    return 'Hello, World!'


class FlaskTestCase(unittest.TestCase):
    def setUp(self):
        self.app = app.test_client()
        self.app.testing = True

    def test_home_route(self):
        response = self.app.get('/')
        self.assertEqual(response.status_code, 200)
        self.assertEqual(response.data, b'Hello, World!')


if __name__ == '__main__':
    unittest.main()
```

- **Testing Routes**

    - o Test various HTTP methods and validate the response:

```python
def test_post_route(self):
    data = {'name': 'Flask'}
    response = self.app.post('/submit', json=data)
    self.assertEqual(response.status_code, 200)
    self.assertIn(b'Success', response.data)
```

    - o

- **Mocking External Services**

- Use libraries like unittest.mock to simulate APIs or database calls:

```python
@patch('app.external_api_call')
def test_external_service(self, mock_api):
    mock_api.return_value = {'status': 'ok'}
    response = self.app.get('/external')
    self.assertEqual(response.json, {'status': 'ok'})
```

- **Testing the Database**

  - Use Flask's **SQLAlchemy** or any ORM testing facilities. Use an in-memory SQLite database for faster and isolated tests:

```python
app.config['SQLALCHEMY_DATABASE_URI'] = 'sqlite:///:memory:'
app.config['SQLALCHEMY_TRACK_MODIFICATIONS'] = False
```

- **Testing Best Practices**

  - **Arrange-Act-Assert Pattern**:

    - Arrange: Set up test data and environment.

    - Act: Perform actions (e.g., make a request).

    - Assert: Verify the results.

  - **Keep Tests Isolated**:

    - Each test should be independent and not affect others.

  - **Use Fixtures**:

    - Simplify test setup and teardown:

```python
@pytest.fixture
def client():
    with app.test_client() as client:
        yield client
```

  - **Coverage Reporting**

    - Use tools like coverage.py to measure test coverage.

  - **Automate Tests**

    - Integrate your tests with CI/CD pipelines using tools like GitHub Actions, Travis CI, or Jenkins.

- **Advanced Topics**

  - **Parameterization with pytest**: Run the same test with different inputs.

  - **Testing Authentication and Authorization**: Test login flows, JWT tokens, and role-based access control.

    o  **Performance Testing**: Use tools like locust or jMeter to evaluate load handling.

# Example:

Here is a complete example of a Flask application with associated unit tests. This includes routes, a database setup, and comprehensive testing. This setup is modular, scalable, and serves as a good starting point for building and testing Flask applications.

- **Flask Application: To-Do App**

    - The application allows users to:

        - View all tasks.

        - Add a new task.

        - Mark a task as completed.

- **Project Structure:**

```
project/
├── app/
│   ├── __init__.py
│   ├── models.py
│   ├── routes.py
├── tests/
│   ├── __init__.py
│   └── test_app.py
└── run.py
```

- **Application Code:**

    - **Application Factory: __init__.py**

```python
from flask import Flask
from flask_sqlalchemy import SQLAlchemy


db = SQLAlchemy()


def create_app():
    app = Flask(__name__)
    app.config['SQLALCHEMY_DATABASE_URI'] = 'sqlite:///test.db'
    app.config['SQLALCHEMY_TRACK_MODIFICATIONS'] = False
    db.init_app(app)


    with app.app_context():
        db.create_all()


    from .routes import main
    app.register_blueprint(main)
```

```
    return app
```

- **Database Models:** models.py

```python
from . import db


class Task(db.Model):
    id = db.Column(db.Integer, primary_key=True)
    title = db.Column(db.String(80), nullable=False)
    completed = db.Column(db.Boolean, default=False)
```

- **Application Routes:** routes.py

```python
from flask import Blueprint, request, jsonify
from .models import Task
from . import db


main = Blueprint('main', __name__)


@main.route('/tasks', methods=['GET'])
def get_tasks():
    tasks = Task.query.all()
    return jsonify([{'id': task.id, 'title': task.title, 'completed': task.completed}
for task in tasks])


@main.route('/tasks', methods=['POST'])
def add_task():
    data = request.json
    if 'title' not in data:
        return jsonify({'error': 'Title is required'}), 400
    task = Task(title=data['title'])
    db.session.add(task)
    db.session.commit()
    return jsonify({'id': task.id, 'title': task.title, 'completed': task.completed}),
201


@main.route('/tasks/<int:task_id>', methods=['PATCH'])
def complete_task(task_id):
    task = Task.query.get(task_id)
    if not task:
        return jsonify({'error': 'Task not found'}), 404
```

```python
        task.completed = True
        db.session.commit()
        return jsonify({'id': task.id, 'title': task.title, 'completed': task.completed})
```

- o **Entry Point:** run.py

```python
from app import create_app


app = create_app()


if __name__ == '__main__':
    app.run(debug=True)
```

- **Test Suite:** test_app.py

```python
import unittest
from app import create_app, db
from app.models import Task


class TestTaskApp(unittest.TestCase):
    @classmethod
    def setUpClass(cls):
        cls.app = create_app()
        cls.app.config['TESTING'] = True
        cls.app.config['SQLALCHEMY_DATABASE_URI'] = 'sqlite:///:memory:'
        cls.client = cls.app.test_client()

        with cls.app.app_context():
            db.create_all()

    @classmethod
    def tearDownClass(cls):
        with cls.app.app_context():
            db.session.remove()
            db.drop_all()

    def test_add_task(self):
        response = self.client.post('/tasks', json={'title': 'Test Task'})
        self.assertEqual(response.status_code, 201)
        data = response.get_json()
        self.assertEqual(data['title'], 'Test Task')
```

```python
        self.assertFalse(data['completed'])

    def test_get_tasks(self):
        # Add a task first
        self.client.post('/tasks', json={'title': 'Task to Get'})
        response = self.client.get('/tasks')
        self.assertEqual(response.status_code, 200)
        data = response.get_json()
        self.assertTrue(any(task['title'] == 'Task to Get' for task in data))

    def test_complete_task(self):
        # Add a task
        response = self.client.post('/tasks', json={'title': 'Task to Complete'})
        task_id = response.get_json()['id']

        # Mark it as completed
        response = self.client.patch(f'/tasks/{task_id}')
        self.assertEqual(response.status_code, 200)
        data = response.get_json()
        self.assertTrue(data['completed'])

    def test_task_not_found(self):
        response = self.client.patch('/tasks/999')
        self.assertEqual(response.status_code, 404)
        data = response.get_json()
        self.assertEqual(data['error'], 'Task not found')


if __name__ == '__main__':
    unittest.main()
```

- **Explanation:**

  - **Application Code:**

    - Database Model: Represents tasks with id, title, and completed attributes.

    - Endpoints:

      - GET /tasks: Retrieves all tasks.

      - POST /tasks: Adds a new task (requires a title).

      - PATCH /tasks/<task_id>: Marks a task as completed.

  - **Test Code:**

- **Setup and Teardown:**

    - setUpClass: Creates an in-memory database for testing.

    - tearDownClass: Drops all tables after tests.

  - **Test Cases:**

    - Verifies functionalities for all endpoints.

    - Tests edge cases, like missing title or nonexistent task IDs.

o **Run:**

  - **Run the Application:**

    - python run.py

  - **Run the Tests:**

    - python -m unittest discover -s tests

```
PS D:\tutorial> .venv\scripts\activate
(.venv) PS D:\tutorial> python -m unittest discover -s tests
.D:\tutorial\app\routes.py:24: LegacyAPIWarning: The Query.get() method is consi
dered legacy as of the 1.x series of SQLAlchemy and becomes a legacy construct i
n 2.0. The method is now available as Session.get() (deprecated since: 2.0) (Bac
kground on SQLAlchemy 2.0 at: https://sqlalche.me/e/b8d9)
  task = Task.query.get(task_id)
...
----------------------------------------------------------------------
Ran 4 tests in 4.075s

OK
(.venv) PS D:\tutorial> []
```

- **Features of This Setup**

  o **Modular Design:** Code is separated into models, routes, and app initialization for clarity.

  o **Testing:** Includes tests for all major features: adding tasks, retrieving tasks, completing tasks, and handling errors.

  o **In-Memory Database:** Ensures the test suite doesn't interfere with the production database.

# 25. Deploy Flask Application

After development and testing, transition from a development environment to a production-ready setup, a Flask application must be deployed on a real web server. Depending on your resources and requirements, there are various options for deploying a Flask web application. For smaller applications, consider using one of the following hosted platforms, which offer free plans suitable for small-scale deployments:

- Heroku

- dotCloud

- WebFaction

Additionally, Flask applications can be deployed on cloud platforms such as Google Cloud. Services like 'localtunnel' allow you to share your local application without dealing with DNS configurations or firewall settings. If you prefer to use a dedicated web server instead of the shared platforms mentioned above, there are several options available for exploration.

## Local Development Access

- **Allow External Access:**

    - Modify app.run() to listen to all IPs:

        - app.run(host="0.0.0.0", port=5000)

    - Find your local IP (e.g., 192.168.1.100) and share the URL

        - http://192.168.1.100:5000

    - Set up firewall rules to allow traffic on port 5000.

- **Tools for Public Access (Optional):**

    - Use ngrok for temporary public URLs

pip install pyngrok

ngrok http 5000

## Deploy on Cloud Platforms

- **Heroku:**

    - **Install Heroku CLI**

        - curl https://cli-assets.heroku.com/install.sh | sh

    - **Prepare Your Project:**

        - Add requirements.txt

- pip freeze > requirements.txt
    - Create a Procfile:
        - web: gunicorn app:app
- **Deploy:**

```
git init

git add .

git commit -m "Deploy Flask App"

heroku create

git push heroku master
```

- **Access Your App**: Heroku will provide a public URL.

- **Google App Engine:**
    - **Install gcloud CLI:**
        - Google App Engine
        - Install gcloud CLI
    - **Prepare Your Project:**
        - Add app.yaml
            - runtime: python
            - entrypoint: gunicorn -w 4 -b :$PORT app:app
        - Add dependencies to requirements.txt.
    - **Deploy:**
        - gcloud app deploy
    - **Access Your App**: Google will provide a public URL.

- **AWS Elastic Beanstalk**
    - **Install EB CLI:**
        - pip install awsebcli
    - **Initialize the Project:**
        - eb init
    - **Deploy:**
        - eb create flask-env
    - **Access Your App**: AWS will provide a public URL.

# Deploy on Virtual Private Servers (VPS)

- **With Gunicorn and Nginx**
  - **Setup Server**
    - Install Python, Pip, and Virtualenv:
      - sudo apt update
      - sudo apt install python3 python3-pip python3-venv
  - **Clone Your Project**:
    - git clone <your-repo>
    - cd <your-repo>
    - python3 -m venv venv
    - source venv/bin/activate
    - pip install -r requirements.txt
  - **Run with Gunicorn**:
    - pip install gunicorn
    - gunicorn -w 4 -b 0.0.0.0:8000 app:app
  - **Set Up Nginx**:
    - **Install Nginx**:
      - sudo apt install nginx
  - **Configure Nginx**:
    - sudo nano /etc/nginx/sites-available/flaskapp
    - **Add**:

```
server {

    listen 80;

    server_name <your_domain_or_IP>;


    location / {

        proxy_pass http://127.0.0.1:8000;

        proxy_set_header Host $host;

        proxy_set_header X-Real-IP $remote_addr;

        proxy_set_header X-Forwarded-For $proxy_add_x_forwarded_for;
```

```
        }

    }
```

- o  **Enable and restart:**

```
sudo ln -s /etc/nginx/sites-available/flaskapp /etc/nginx/sites-enabled

sudo systemctl restart nginx
```

## Docker Deployment

- **Create a Dockerfile:**

```
FROM python:3.9-slim

WORKDIR /app

COPY . /app

RUN pip install -r requirements.txt

CMD ["python", "app.py"]
```

- **Build and Run the Container:**

```
docker build -t flask-app .

docker run -p 5000:5000 flask-app
```

- **Access Your App:** Visit http://localhost:5000.


# Serverless Deployment

- **AWS Lambda (Using Zappa):**
  - o  **Install Zappa:**
    - pip install zappa
  - o  **Initialize Zappa:**
    - zappa init
  - o  **Deploy:**
    - zappa deploy
  - o  **Access Your App:**
    - Zappa will provide a public URL.